HIGH WYCOMBE

AMERSHAM · CHESHAM · GERRARDS CROSS · BEACONSFIELD
MARLOW · BOURNE END · GT. MISSENDEN · THE CHALFONTS

D1742337

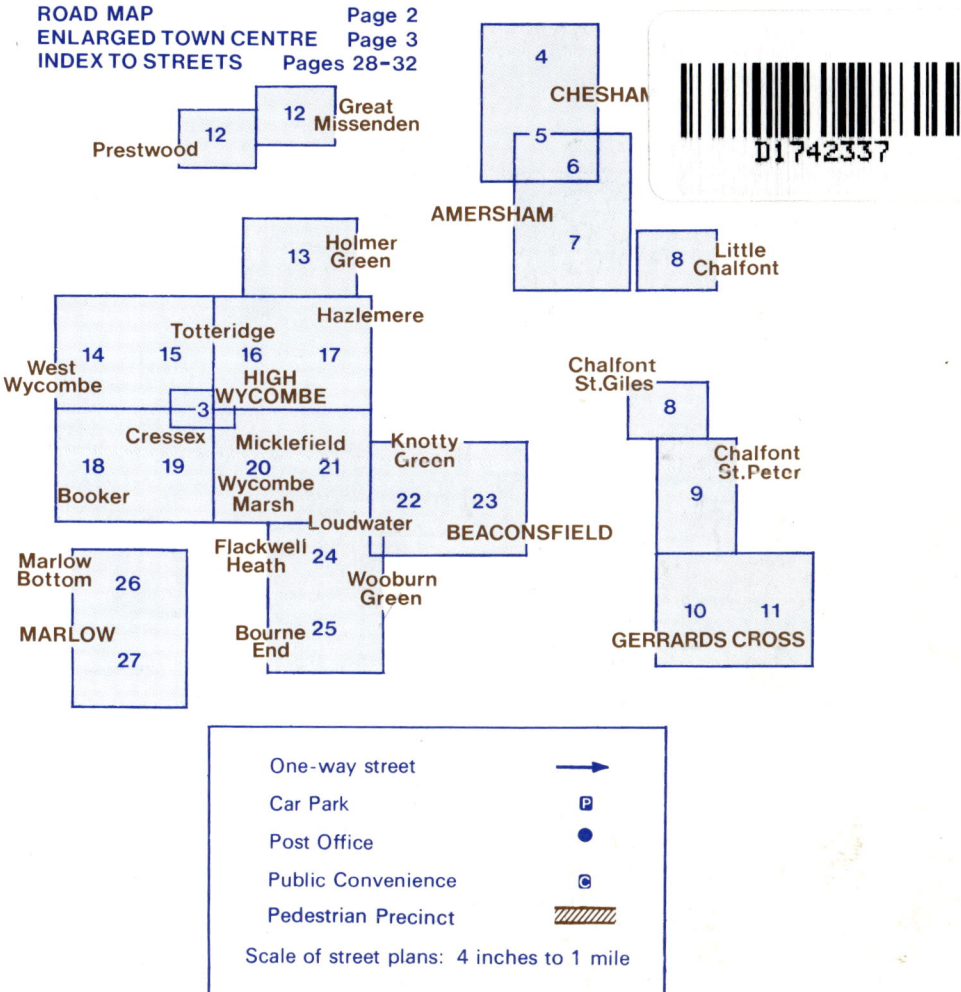

One-way street	→
Car Park	P
Post Office	●
Public Convenience	C
Pedestrian Precinct	▨

Scale of street plans: 4 inches to 1 mile

Street plans prepared and published by ESTATE PUBLICATIONS, Bridewell House, Tenterden, Kent and based upon the ORDNANCE SURVEY maps with the sanction of the controller of H.M. Stationery Office.

The publishers acknowledge the co-operation of Wycombe, Chiltern and South Bucks District Councils in the preparation of these maps. Every effort has been made to ensure the greatest possible accuracy and the publishers welcome any information that will improve their usefulness.

ISBN 0 86084 371 8

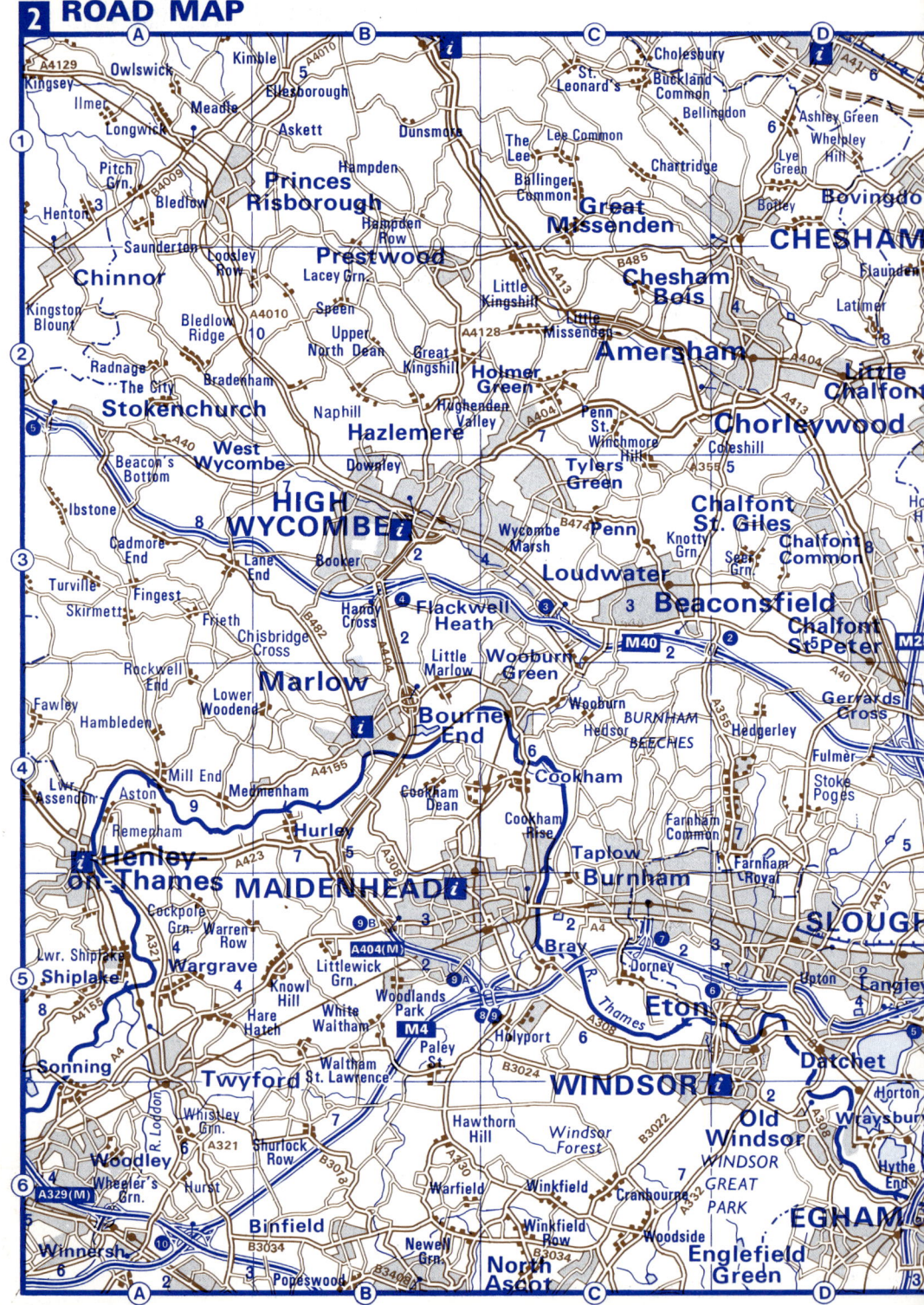

Scale : 8 inches to 1 mile

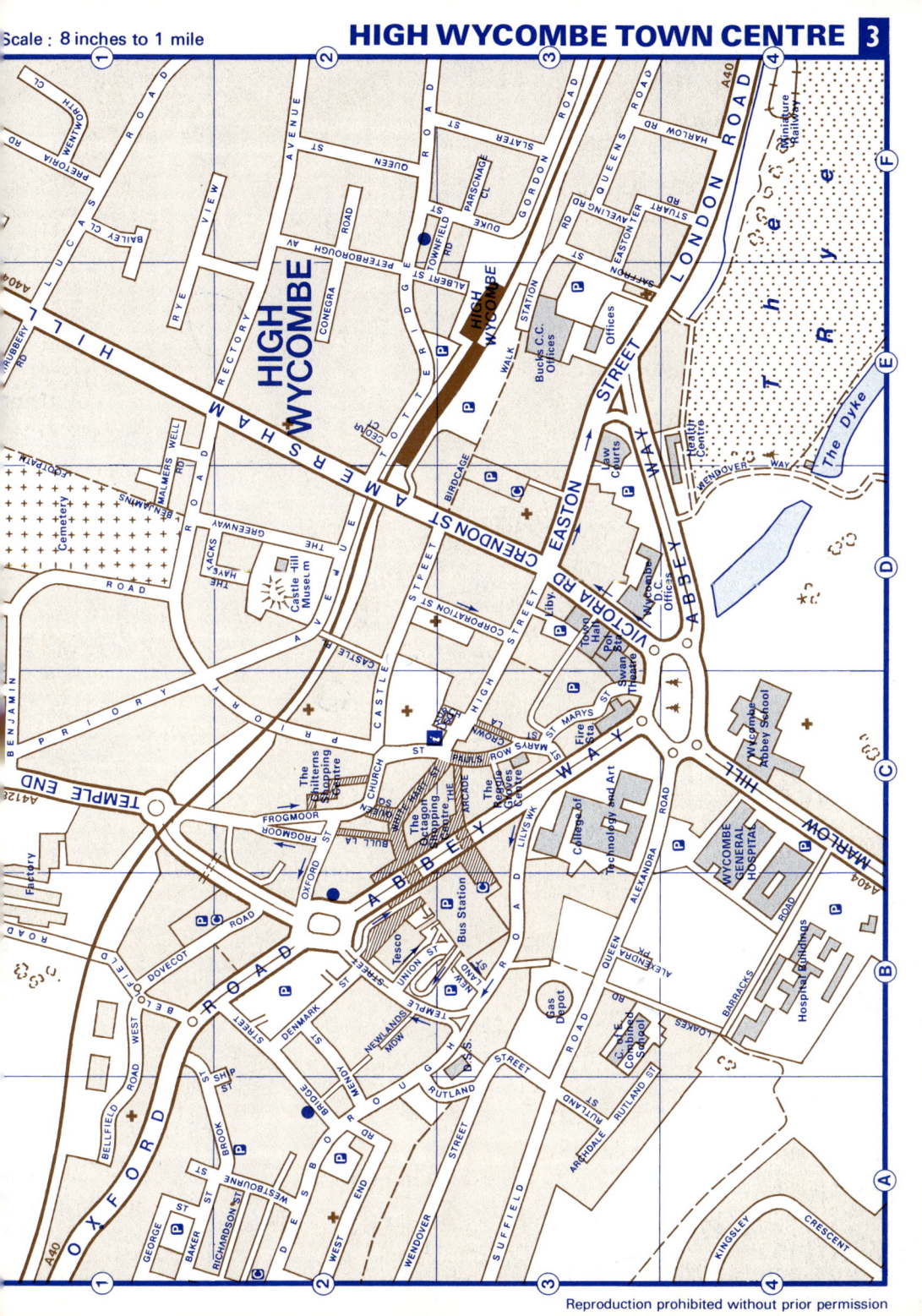

HIGH WYCOMBE

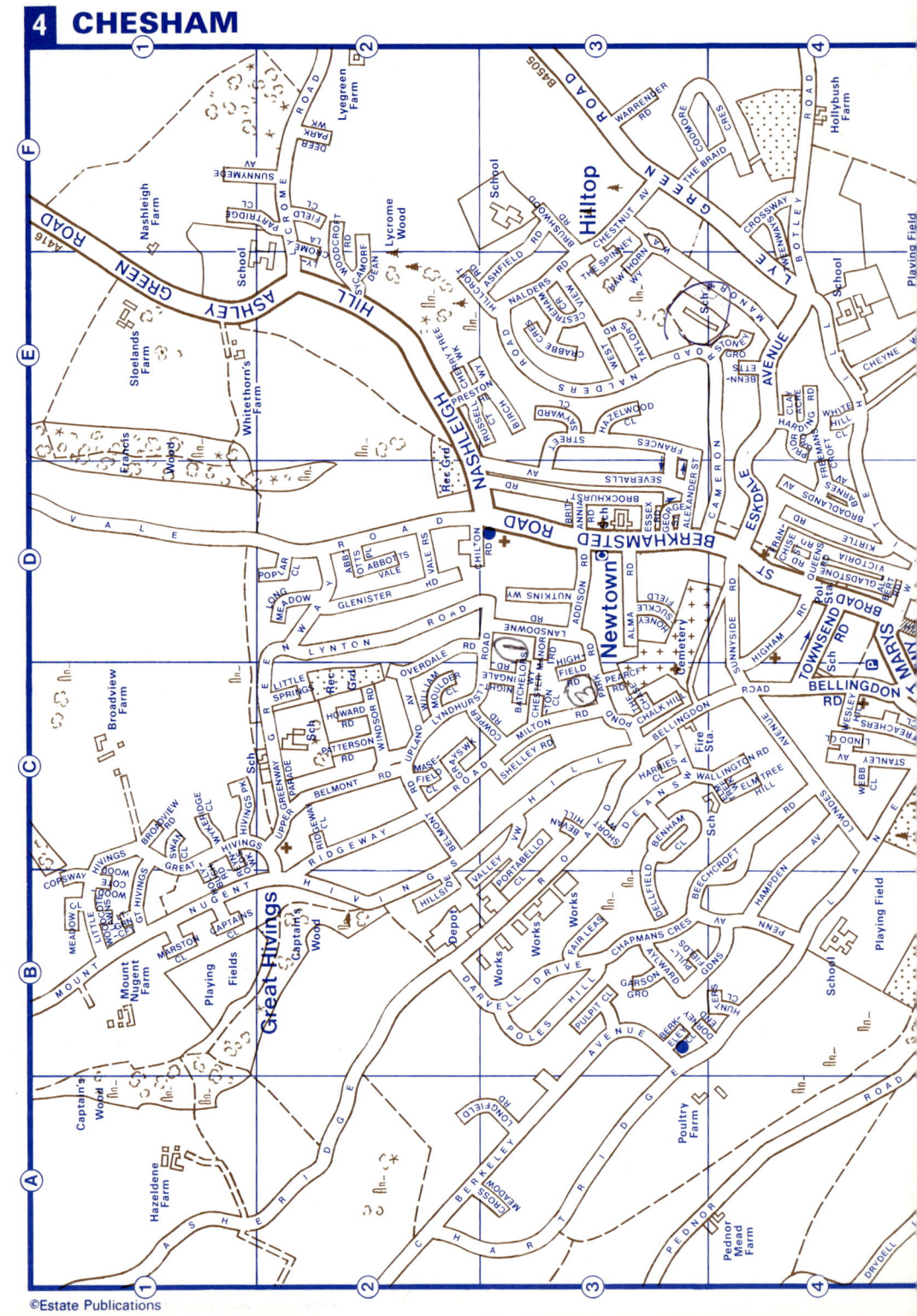

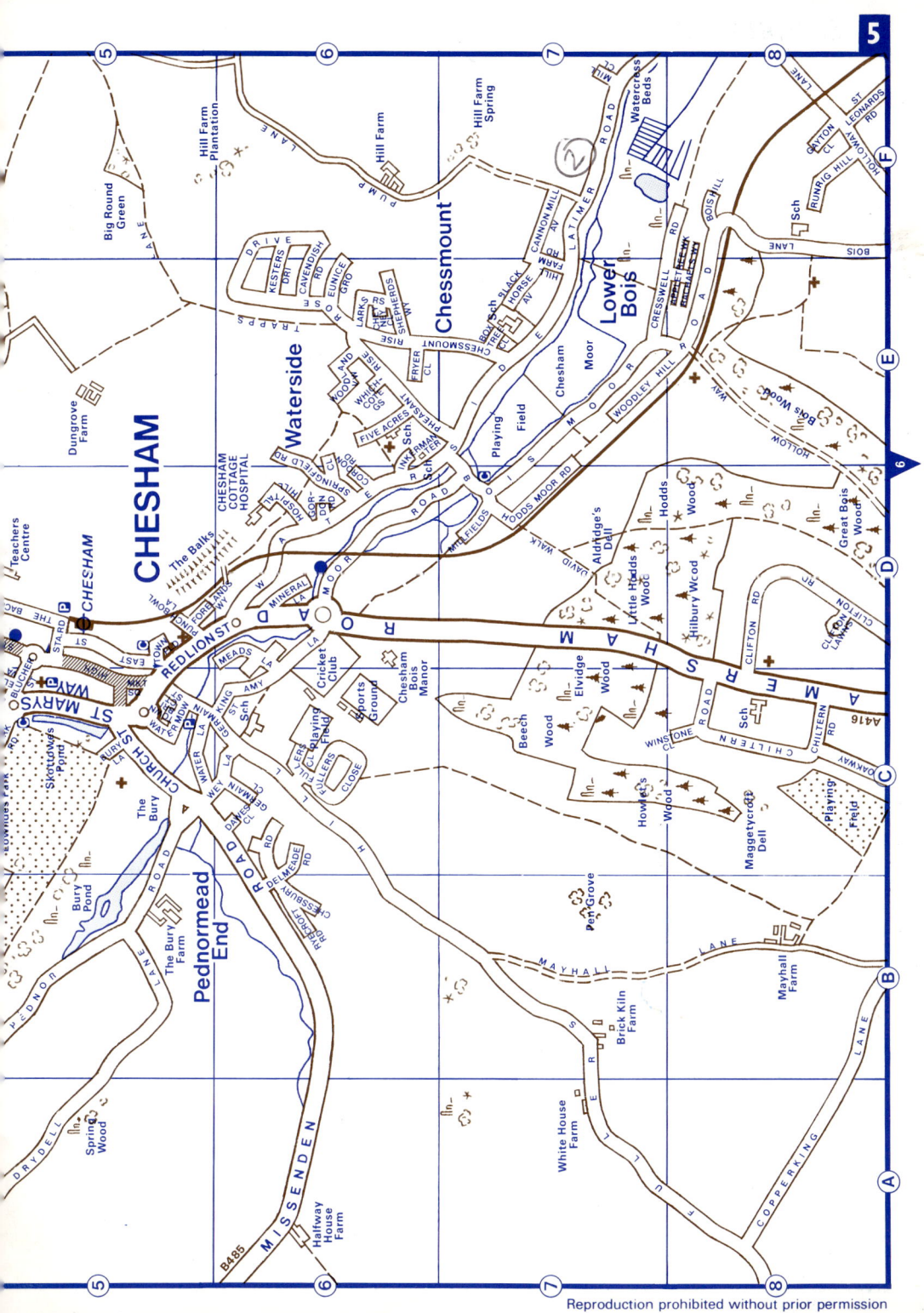

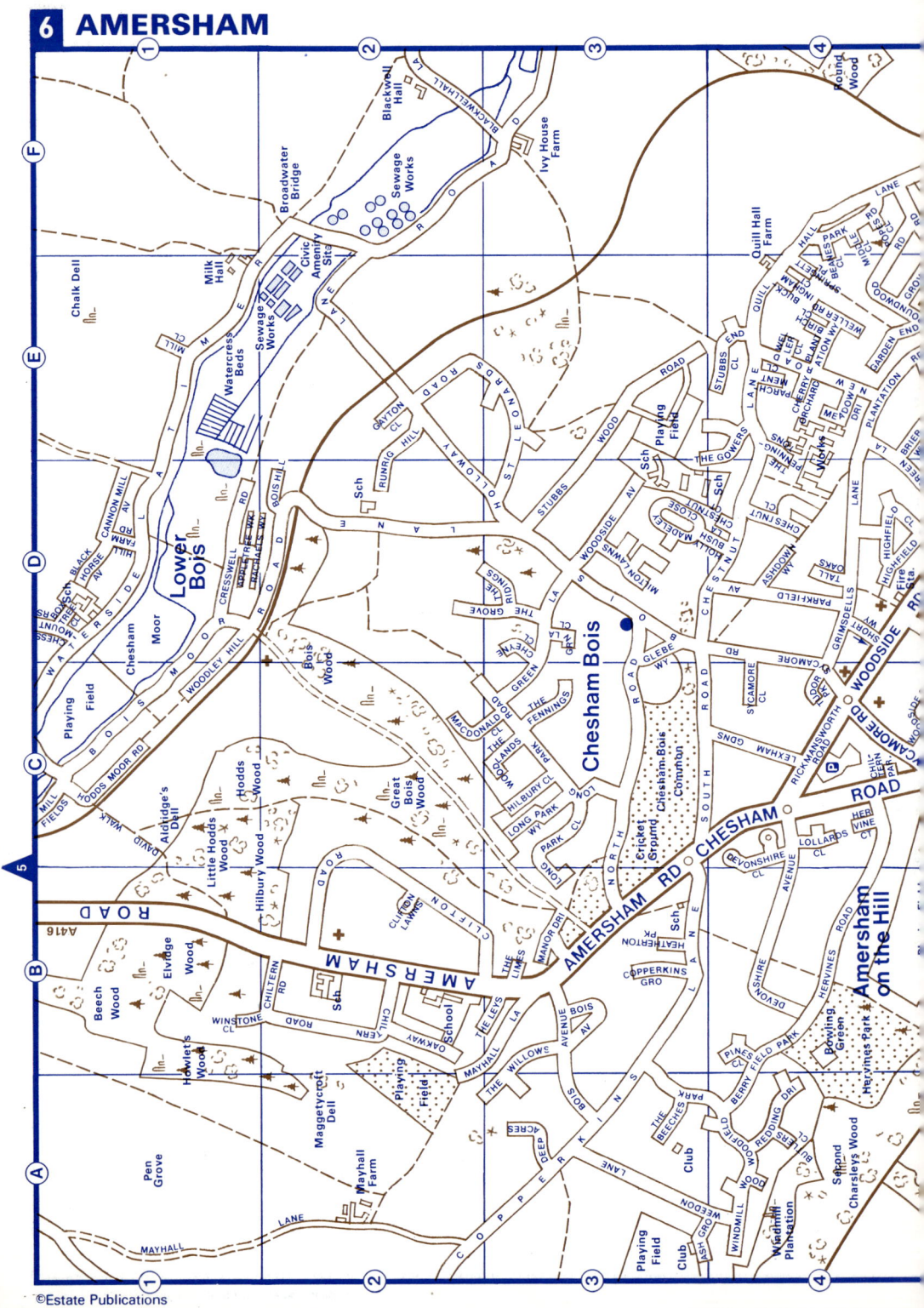

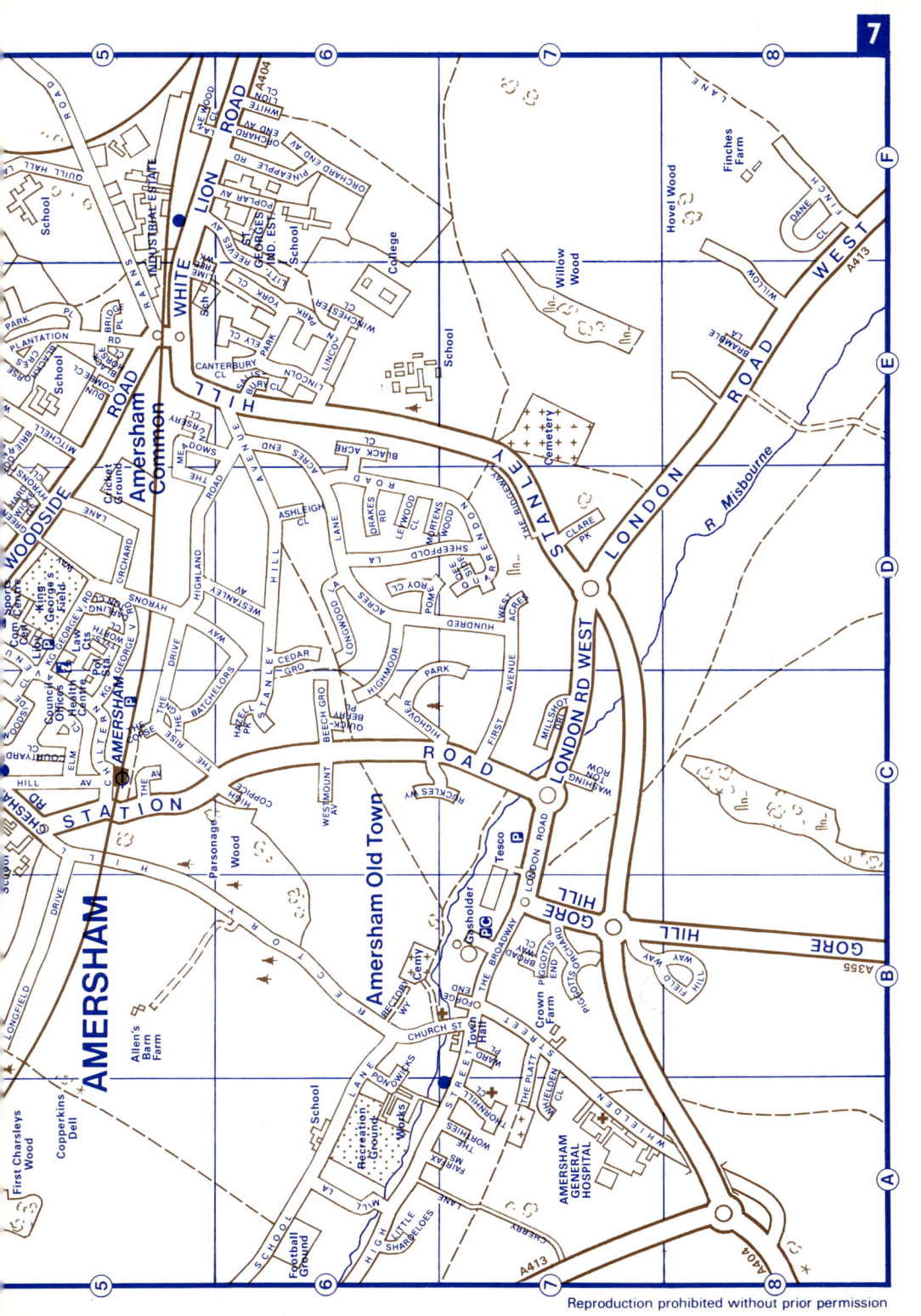

LITTLE CHALFONT

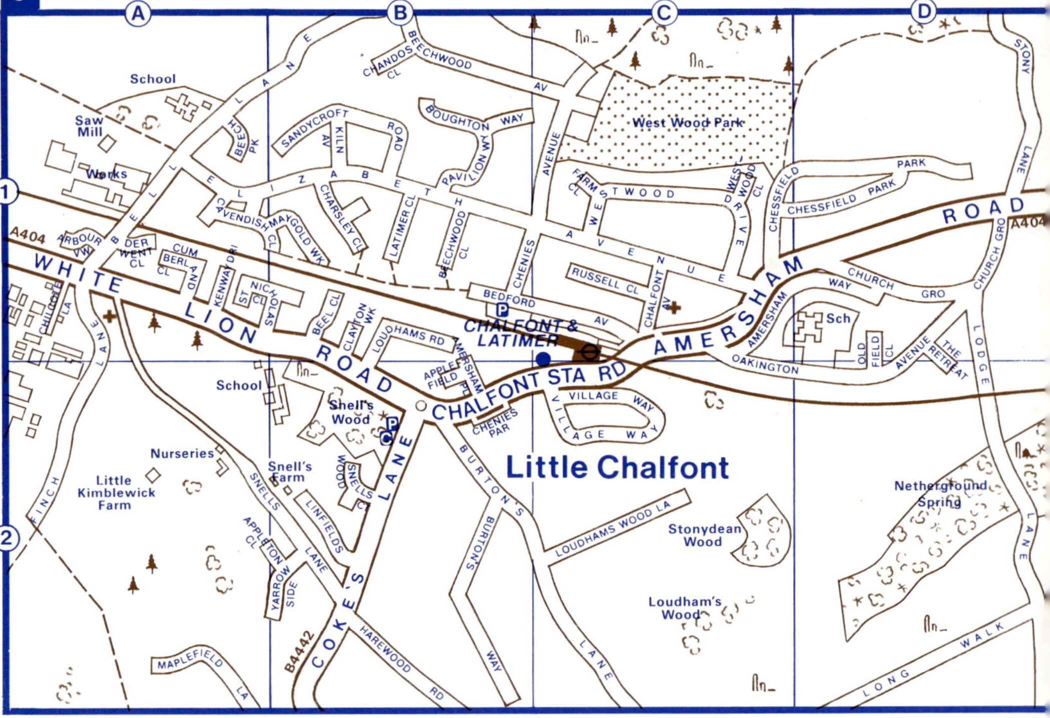

School
Saw Mill
Works
School
BEECHWOOD CL
CHANDOS
BEECHWOOD AV
BOUGHTON WAY
LANE
BEECH
BEECH PK
SANDYCROFT AV
KILN RD
PAVILION WY
AVENUE
West Wood Park
WESTWOOD
WEST DRIVE
CHESSFIELD PARK
CHESSFIELD PARK
STONY LANE
ROAD
A404

A404 WHITE LION ROAD
ARBOUR VW
DER WENT
CUMBERLD
KENWAD DR
NICOLAS CL
CLAYTON WY
CHARSLEY RD
LATIMER CL
MARGOLD WK
BEEL CL
CHENIES
BEECHWOOD CL
BEDFORD
RUSSELL CL
CHALFONT
FARMWOOD
AV
CHENIES
AMERSHAM
Sch
CHURCH WAY
GRO
FIELD
OLD
OAKINGTON
AVENUE
THE RETREAT
LODGE
CHURCH GRO

WHITE LION ROAD
FINCH LANE
CHILTY
VILLA
School
Shell's Wood
LOUDHAMS RD
APPLEFIELD
CHALFONT STA RD
CHENIES PAR
CHALFONT & LATIMER
VILLAGE WAY
VILLAGE WAY
AMERSHAM
Netherground Spring
THE LANE

Nurseries
Little Kimblewick Farm
Snell's Farm
SNELLS CL
COKES LANE
APPLETON
SNELLS LANE
LINFIELDS
WOODS CL
BURTONS LANE
BURROWS WAY
Little Chalfont
Stonydean Wood
Loudhams Wood
LOUDHAMS WOOD LA
LONG WALK

YARROW SIDE
MAPLEFIELD LA
B4442
HAREWOOD RD

CHALFONT ST. GILES

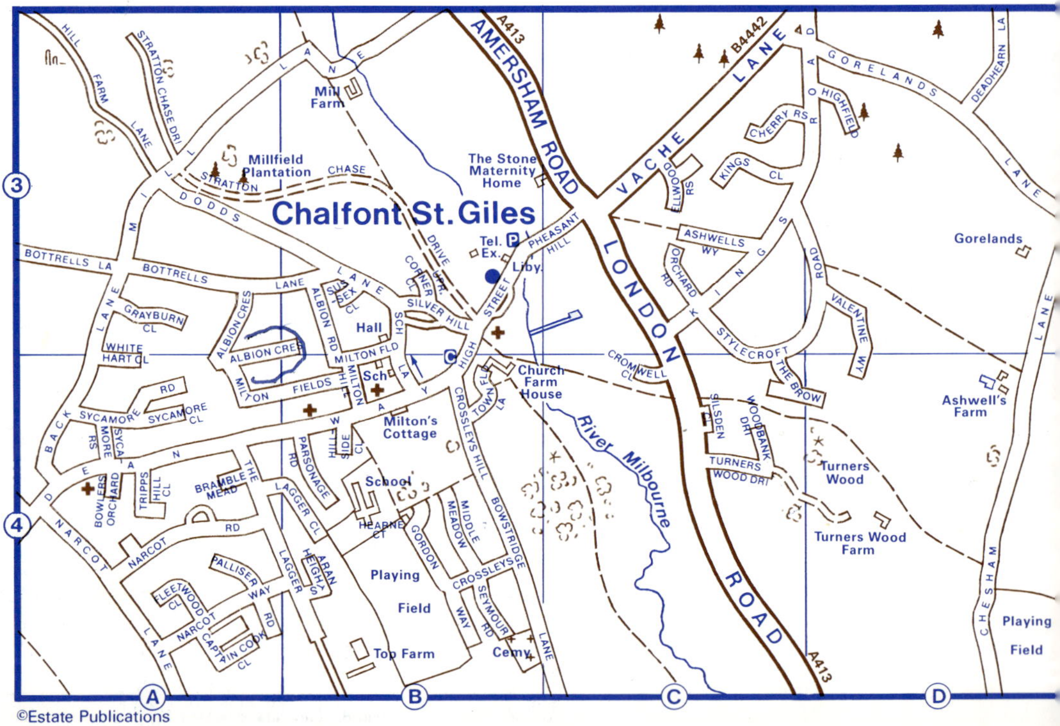

HILL FARM
STRATION CHASE DRI
LANE
Mill Farm
AMERSHAM ROAD
A413
B4442
VACHE LANE
GORELANDS LANE
HIGHFIELD
DEADHEARN LA
Millfield Plantation
STRATION CHASE
The Stone Maternity Home
CHERRY RS
KINGS CL
GORELANDS
Gorelands

BOTTRELLS LA
DODDS
STRATION
Chalfont St. Giles
Tel. Ex.
Lby.
PHEASANT HILL
ASHWELLS
ASHWELLS WY
ORCHARD RD
GOODWYN
VALENTINE WY
STYLECROFT
THE BROW
Ashwell's Farm

GRAYBURN CL
BOTTRELLS LANE
ALBION CRES
ALBION RD
ALBION CRES
Hall
CORNER BEX
DRIVE
SILVER HILL
MILTON FLD
HIGH STREET
CROMWELL
LONDON ROAD
WOODBANK
TURNERS WOOD DRI
Turners Wood
Turners Wood Farm

WHITE HART CL
MILTON FIELDS
Sch
Church Farm House
CROSSLEYS HILL
River Milbourne

SYCAMORE RD
SYCAMORE CL
BRAMBLE MEAD
PARSONAGE CL
Milton's Cottage
School
HEARNE
GORDON
MIDDLE MEADOW
BOWSTRIDGE LANE
SEYMOUR WAY
SILSDEN
TURNERS
Playing Field

BOWERS ORCHARD
TRIPPS HILL CL
EXCAL
NARCOT
FLEETWOOD WAY
PALLISER WAY
NARCOT LANE
LAGGER CL
LAGGER RD
ARAN HGTS
Playing Field
Top Farm
Cemy
A413
CHESHAM ROAD
Playing Field

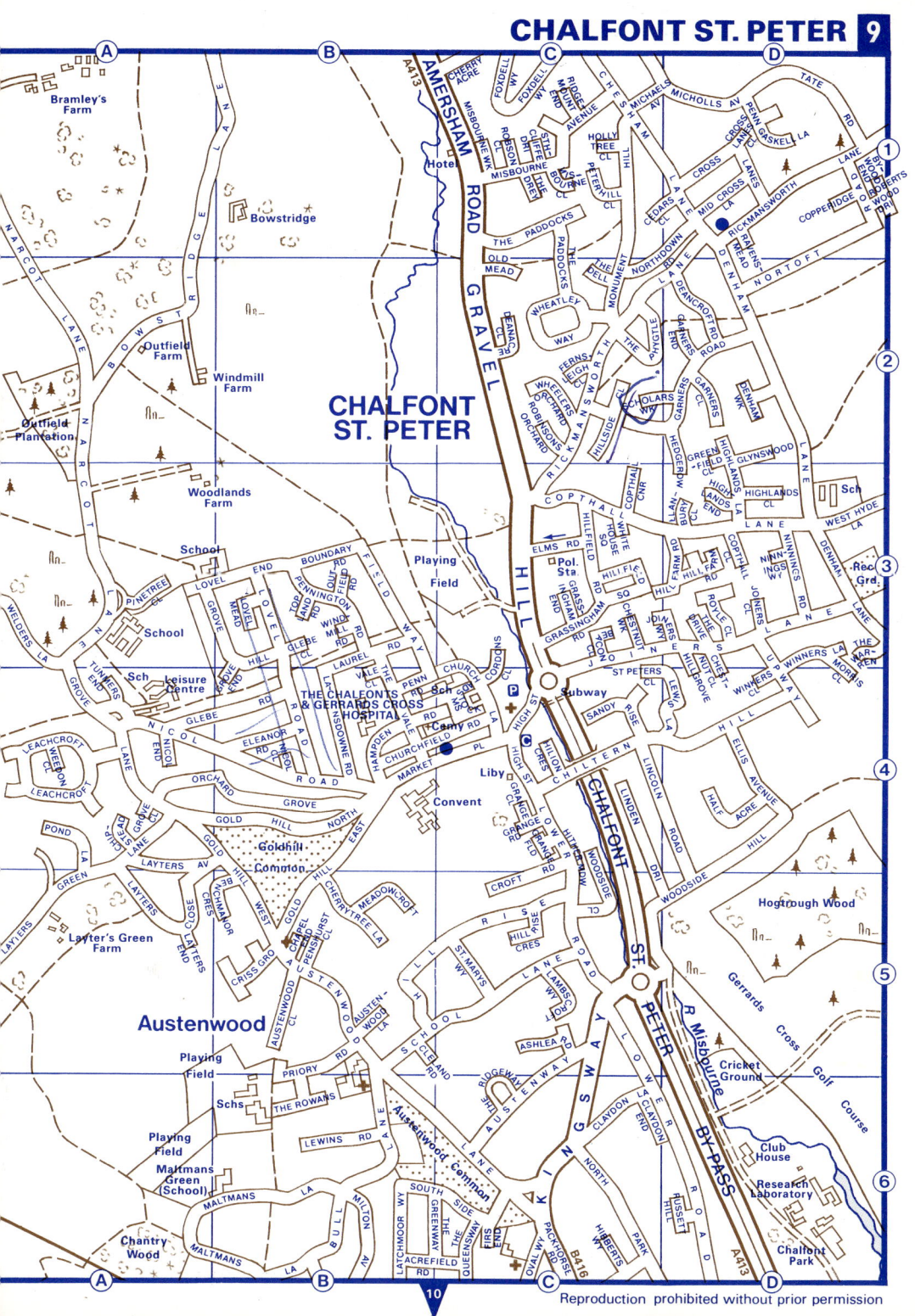

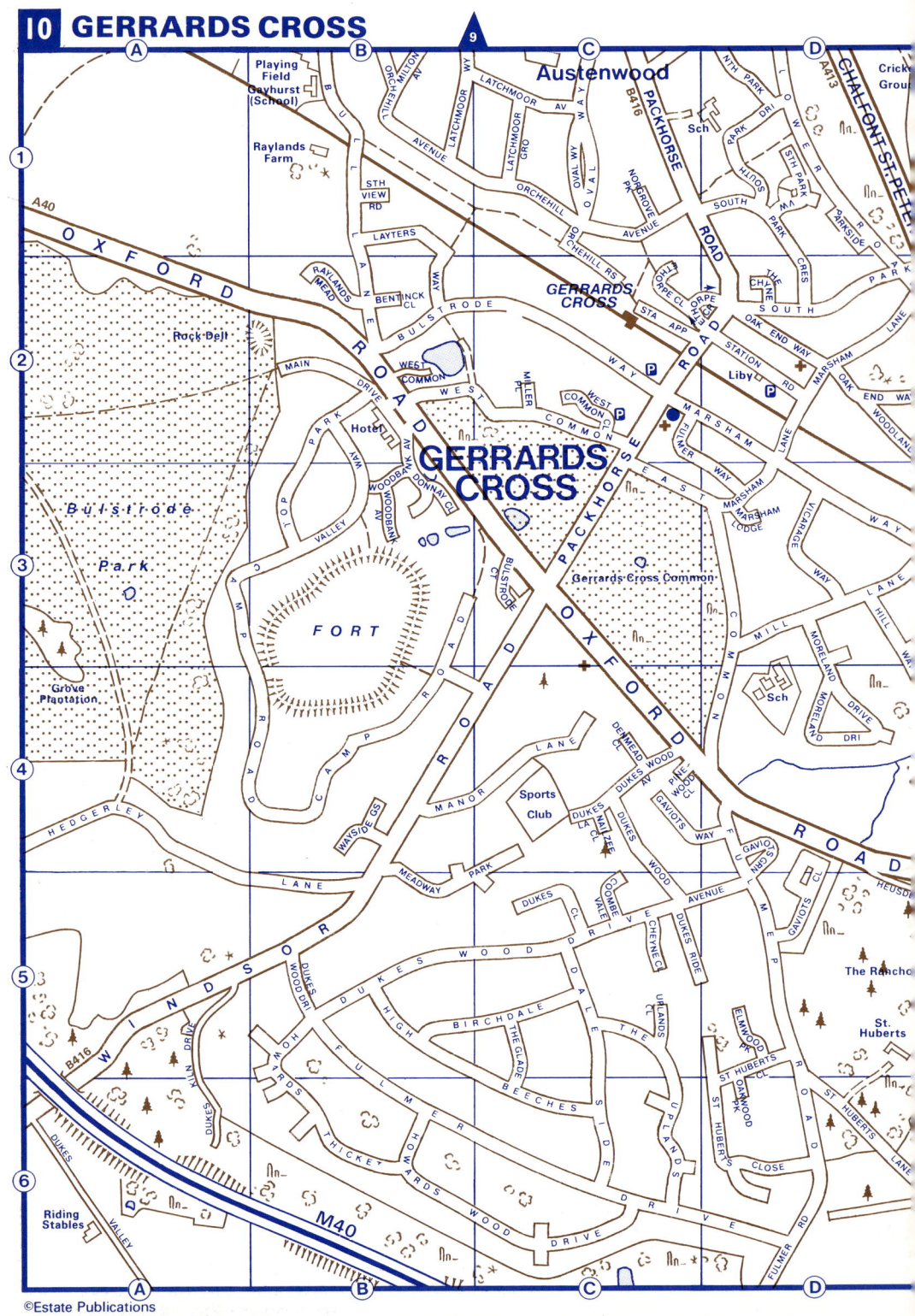

9

A   B   C   D

Playing Field
Gayhurst (School)

Austenwood

Raylands Farm

OXFORD

A40

Rock Dell

Bulstrode

Park

Grove Plantation

FORT

GERRARDS CROSS

West Common

West Common

Hotel

Gerrards Cross Common

PACKHORSE

OXFORD

ROAD

WINDSOR

ROAD

Sports Club

Manor Park

Meadway

Dukes Wood

Birchdale

The Rancho

St. Huberts

Riding Stables

M40

ROAD

©Estate Publications

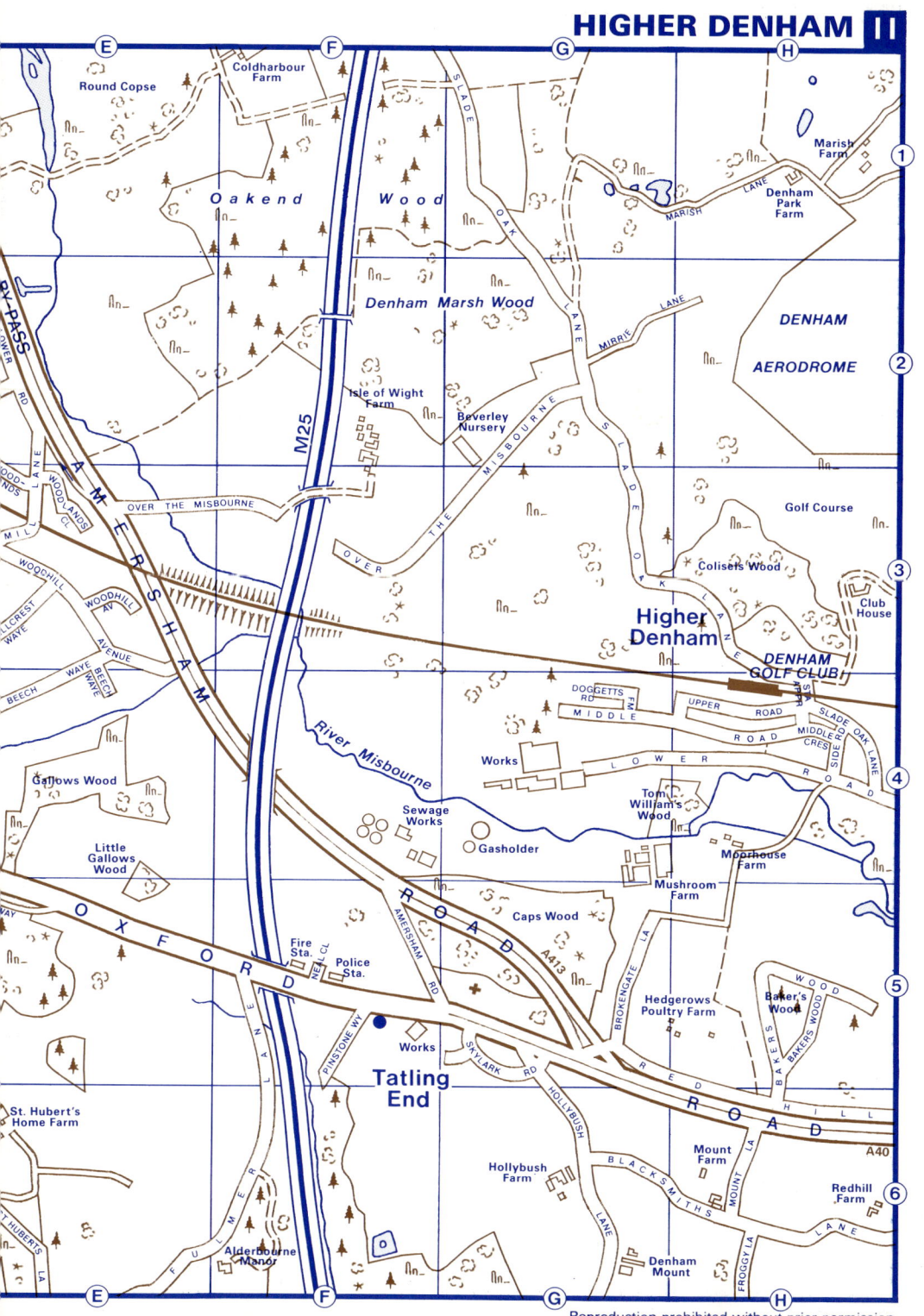

Round Copse
Coldharbour Farm
Marish Farm
Denham Park Farm
MARISH LANE
O a k e n d   W o o d
Denham Marsh Wood
DENHAM AERODROME
Isle of Wight Farm
Beverley Nursery
M25
OVER THE MISBOURNE
Golf Course
Coliseis Wood
Club House
OVER THE MISBOURNE
A M E R S H A M
BY-PASS
TOWER RD
MILL LANE
WOODLANDS CL
WOODHILL
HILLCREST WAYE
WOODHILL AV
AVENUE
BEECH WAYE
BEECH
WAYE
Higher Denham
DENHAM GOLF CLUB
SLADE OAK LANE
River Misbourne
Gallows Wood
DOGGETTS RD
FM
MIDDLE
UPPER   ROAD   MIDDLE
SLADE OAK LANE
CRESC
Little Gallows Wood
Works
LOWER   ROAD
Tom William's Wood
Sewage Works
Gasholder
Moorhouse Farm
Mushroom Farm
Caps Wood
OXFORD
ROAD
AMERSHAM RD
NEEL CL
Fire Sta.
Police Sta.
A413
Hedgerows Poultry Farm
BROKENGATE LA
Baker's Wood
WOOD
BAKERS WOOD
Works
Tatling End
SKYLARK RD
PINSTONE WY
St. Hubert's Home Farm
FULMER LANE
RED HILL
BAKERS
Hollybush Farm
HOLLYBUSH
BLACKSMITHS LANE
Mount Farm
MOUNT LA
ROAD
A40
Redhill Farm
Alderbourne Manor
Denham Mount
FROGGY LA
ST. HUBERT'S LA

E F G H

1 2 3 4 5 6

PRESTWOOD

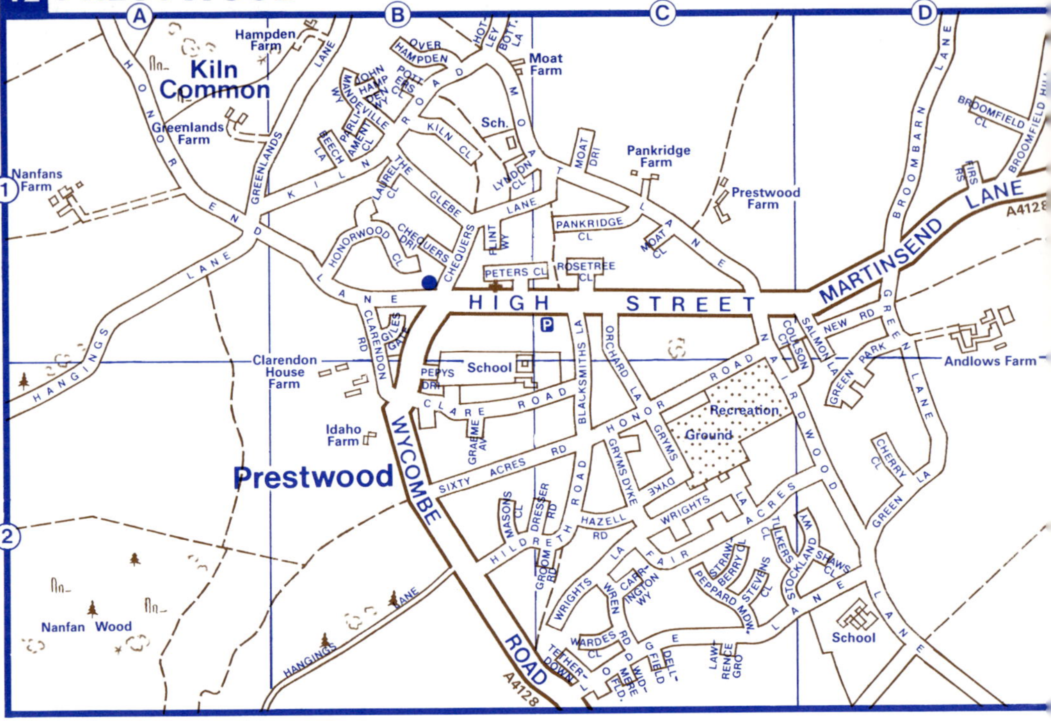

Kiln Common

Hampden Farm
Greenlands Farm
Nanfans Farm
Over Hampden
Moat Farm
Sch.
Pankridge Farm
Prestwood Farm
MARTINSEND LANE
A4128
BROOMFIELD CL
BROOMFIELD HILL
HONOR END LANE
GREENLANDS
KILN LANE
JOHN HAMPDEN WAY
MANDEVILLE
AMERSHAM RD
BEECH CL
LAUREL CL
THE GLEBE
KILN CL
LYNDON
MOAT DRI
HAMPDEN RD
HOTLEY BOTTOM LANE
PANKRIDGE CL
ROSETREE CL
FLINT CL
CHEQUERS DRI
HONORWOOD
CLARENDON
PETERS CL
HIGH STREET
MOAT CL
NAIRDWOOD LANE
COLLSON
SALMON LANE
NEW RD
GREEN PARK
GREEN LANE
Andlows Farm
Clarendon House Farm
School
PEPYS DRI
CLARE ROAD
GRAEME AVE
BLACKSMITHS LA
ORCHARD LANE
HONOR RD
Recreation Ground
CHERRY CL
Idaho Farm
Prestwood
SIXTY ACRES RD
MASONS CL
HILDRETH
BROOM DRESSER RD
WRIGHTS CL
HAZEL RD
GRYMS DYKE
WRIGHTS
CARRINGTON WY
WREN CL
PEPPARD CL
FAIR LA
STRAWBERRY CL
STEVENS
MOAT WAY
STOCKING LA
LIM SHAWS LA
SHAWS CL
GREEN LA
School
WYCOMBE ROAD
HANGINGS LANE
Nanfan Wood
WARDES CL
TERREY DOWN
DELL FIELD
IDELL
LAWRENCE GRO
A4128

GREAT MISSENDEN

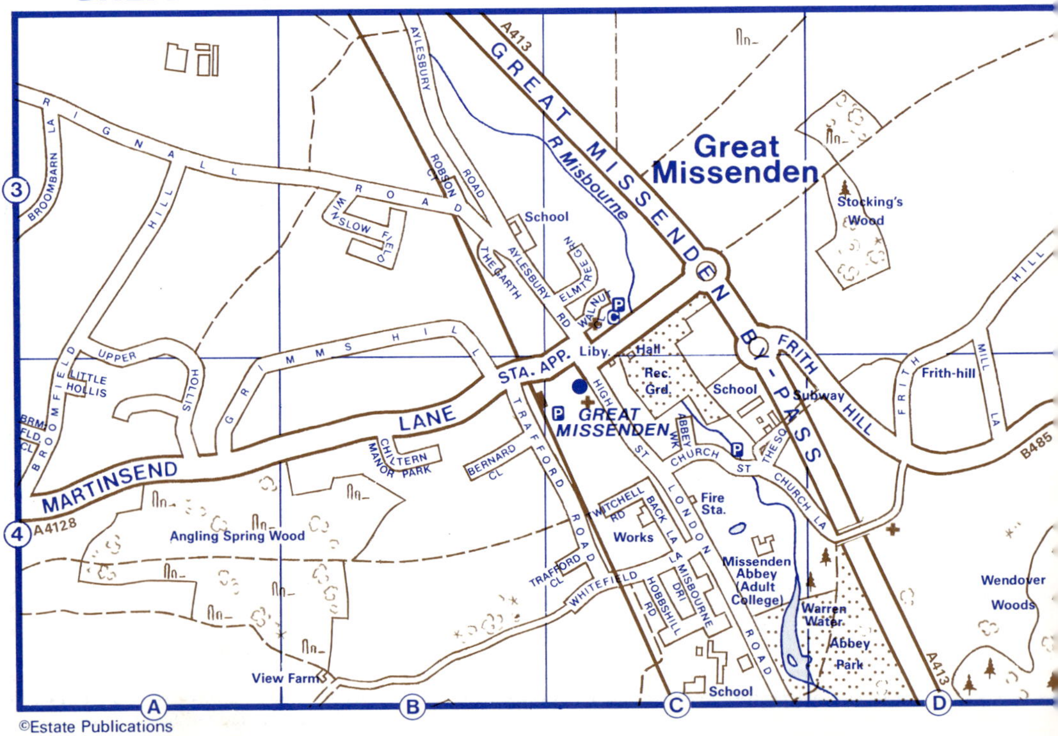

A413
GREAT MISSENDEN BY-PASS
AYLESBURY
Great Missenden
Stocking's Wood
RIGNALL ROAD
HILL
WINSLOW FIELD
ROBSON ROAD
Misbourne
School
AYLESBURY RD
HELGARTH
ELMTREE
WALNUT
STA. APP.
Liby.
Hall
Rec. Grd.
School
FRITH HILL
Frith-hill
FRITH MILL LA
B485
BROOMFIELD
UPPER HOLLIS
LITTLE HOLLIS
GRIMMS HILL
HOLLIS
MARTINSEND LANE
A4128
Angling Spring Wood
CHILTERN MANOR PARK
BERNARD CL
TRAFFORD ROAD
GREAT MISSENDEN
HIGH ST
LONDON RD
ABBEY
CHURCH
Fire Sta.
THE SQUARE
CHURCH LA
Subway
School
WITCHELL
BACK LA
Works
WHITEFIELD RD
HOBBSHILL RD
MISBOURNE
Missenden Abbey (Adult College)
Warren Water
Abbey Park
Wendover Woods
View Farms
School
A413

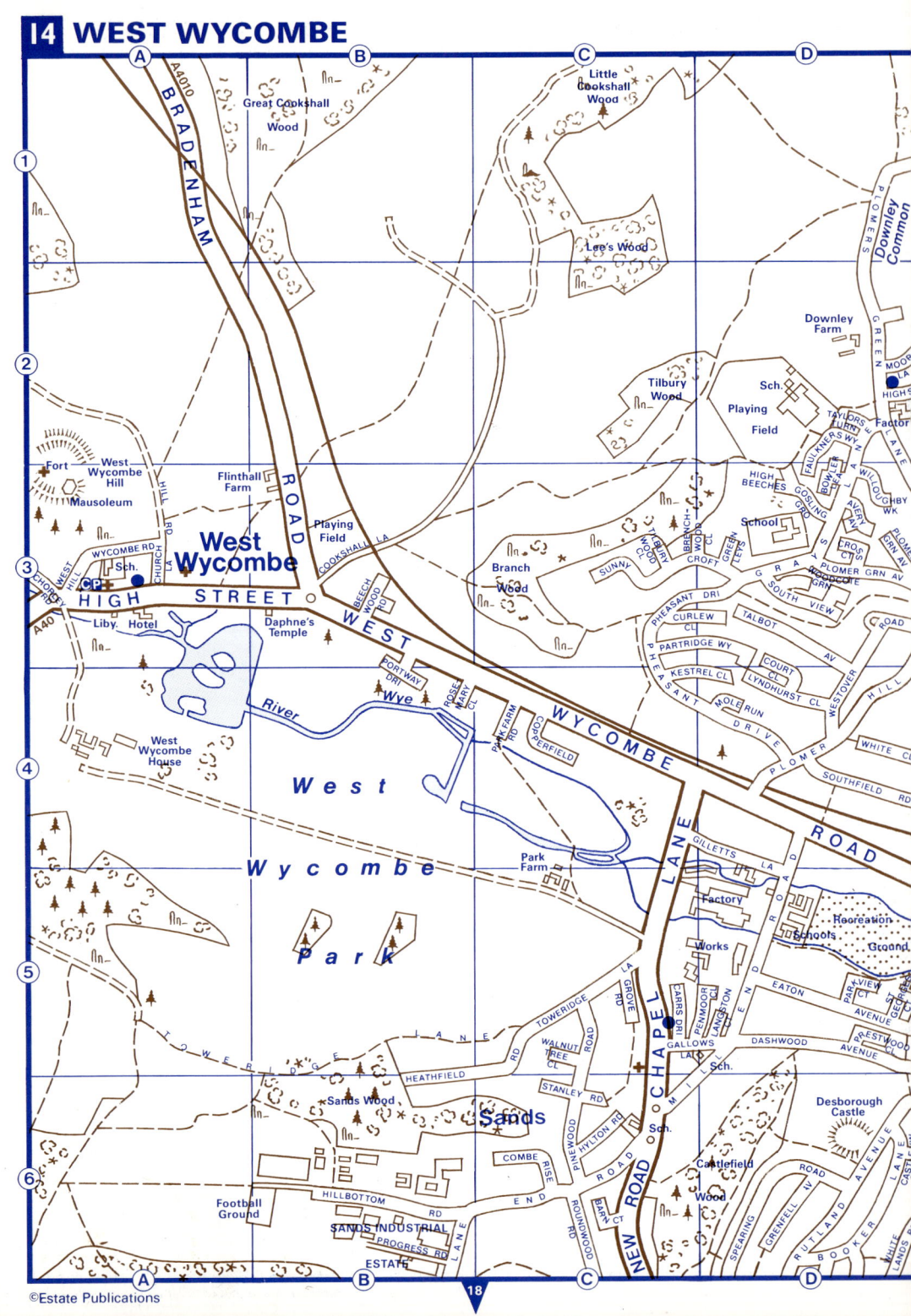

WEST WYCOMBE

BRADENHAM ROAD

A4010

Great Cookshall Wood

Little Cookshall Wood

Lee's Wood

Downley Common

GREEN MOOR LA

HIGH S

Downley Farm

Tilbury Wood

Sch.

Playing Field

TAYLORS TURN

Factor

FAULKNERS WYZ

BOWER LA

WILLOUGHBY WK

HIGH BEECHES

GOSLING GRO

CROSS OAK

BRN AV

PLOM

Fort

West Wycombe Hill

Mausoleum

Flinthall Farm

Playing Field

Branch Wood

School

CROFT

GREEN LETS

TIBURY WOOD

BRANCH WOOD

SUNNY

PLOMER GRN

WOODCOTE

PLOMER GRN LA

SOUTH VIEW

WYCOMBE RD

West Wycombe

Sch.

CP

Liby. Hotel

Daphne's Temple

HIGH STREET

WEST

BEECH WOOD RD

COOKSHALL LA

CHURCH HILL

WEST HILL

A40

CHORLEY RD

River Wye

WYCOMBE

PEASANT DRI

CURLEW

TALBOT

KESTREL CL

COURT CL

LYNDHURST CL

PARTRIDGE WY

PHEASANT

PORTWAY DRI

ROSE

MARY CL

PARK FARM RD

COPP

OVERFIELD

MOLE RUN

WESTOVER HILL

DRIVE

WHITE CL

West Wycombe House

West Wycombe

Park Farm

LANE

GILLETTS LA

PLOMER

SOUTHFIELD RD

ROAD

Factory

Recreation Ground

Wycombe

Park

Works

Schools

TOWERIDGE LANE

GROVE RD

WALNUT TREE CL

PENMOOR CL

LANGSTON CL

EATON AVENUE

PARK VIEW CT

DASHWOOD AVENUE

PRESTWOOD

CARRS DRI

GALLOWS LA

Sch.

Sands Wood

HEATHFIELD

STANLEY RD

Sands

PINEWOOD

HYLTON RD

Sch.

Desborough Castle

Castlefield Wood

SPEARING

GREENFELL AV

RUTLAND AV

BOOKER LANE

CASTLE

Football Ground

HILLBOTTOM RD

SANDS INDUSTRIAL

PROGRESS RD

ESTATE

COMBE RISE

END

LANE

BARN CT

ROUNDWOOD

MILL RD

NEW ROAD

CHAPEL

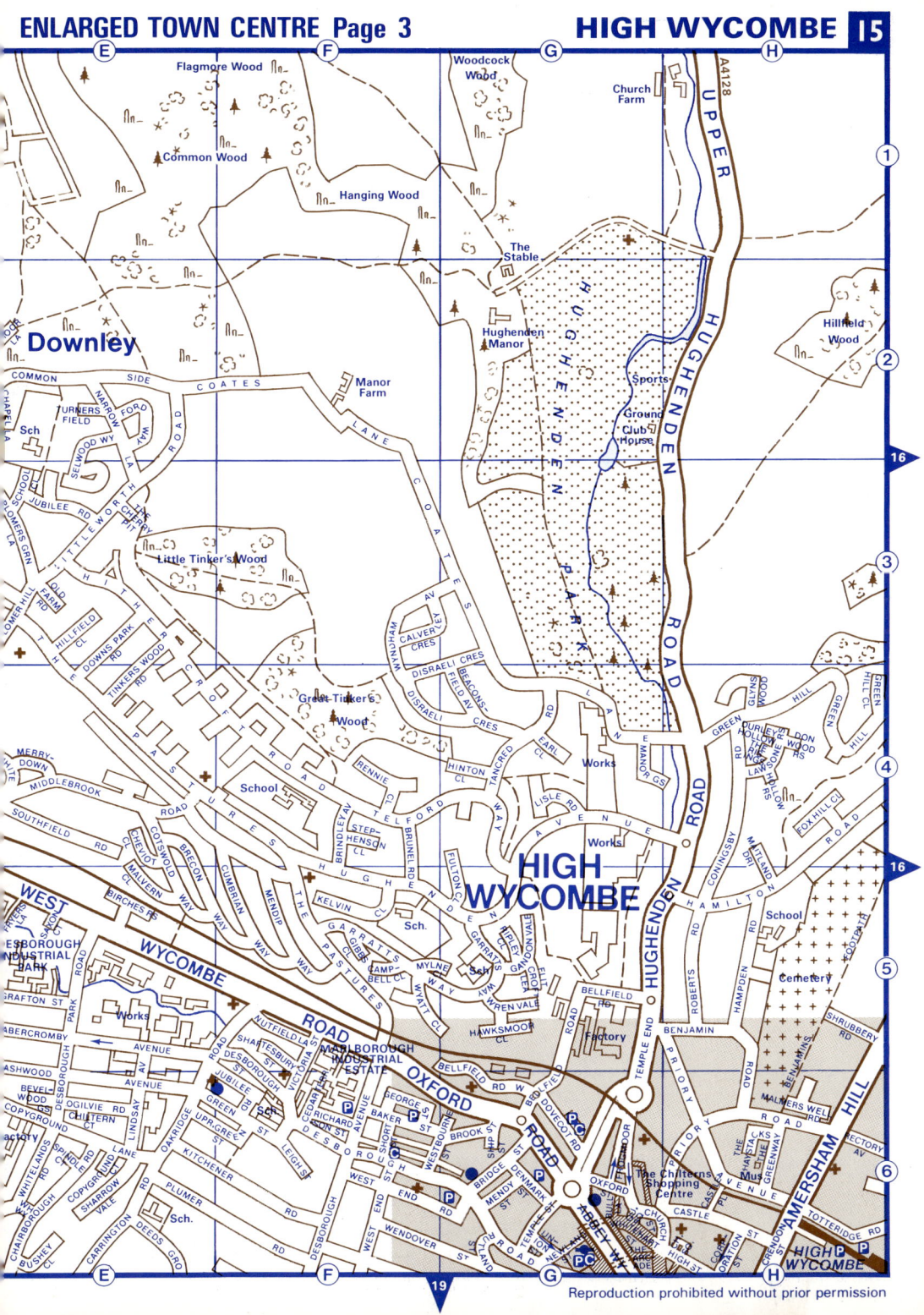

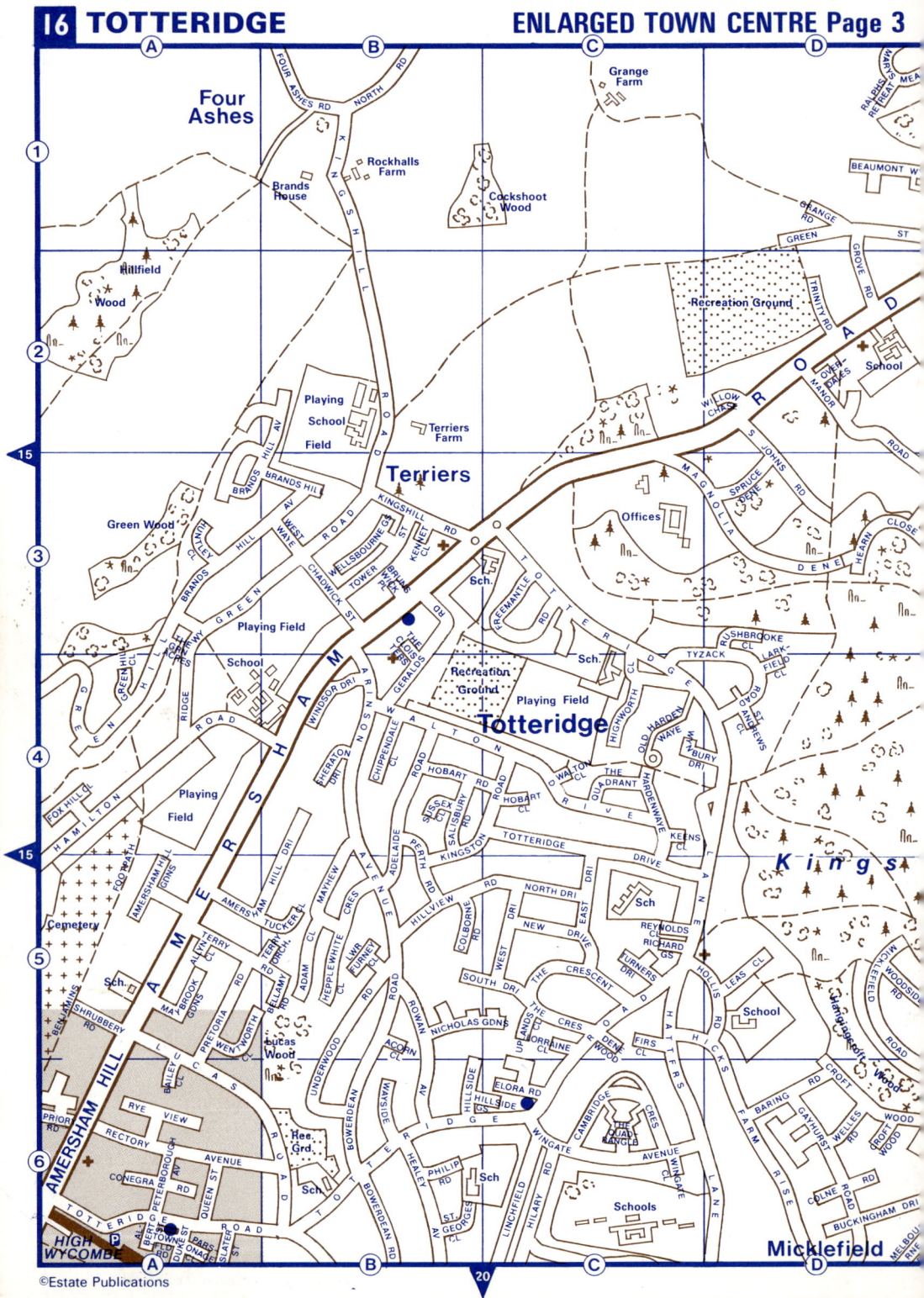

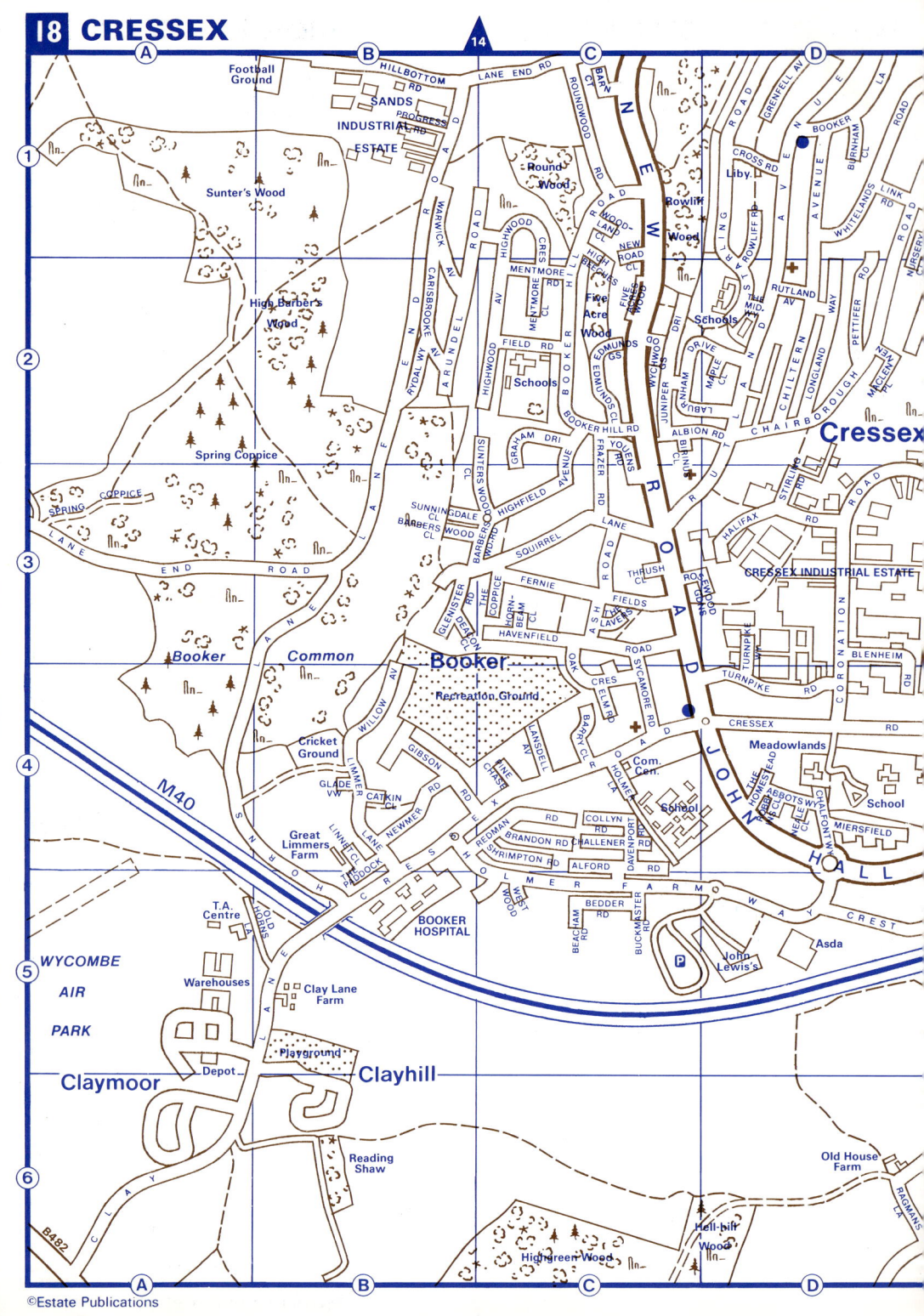

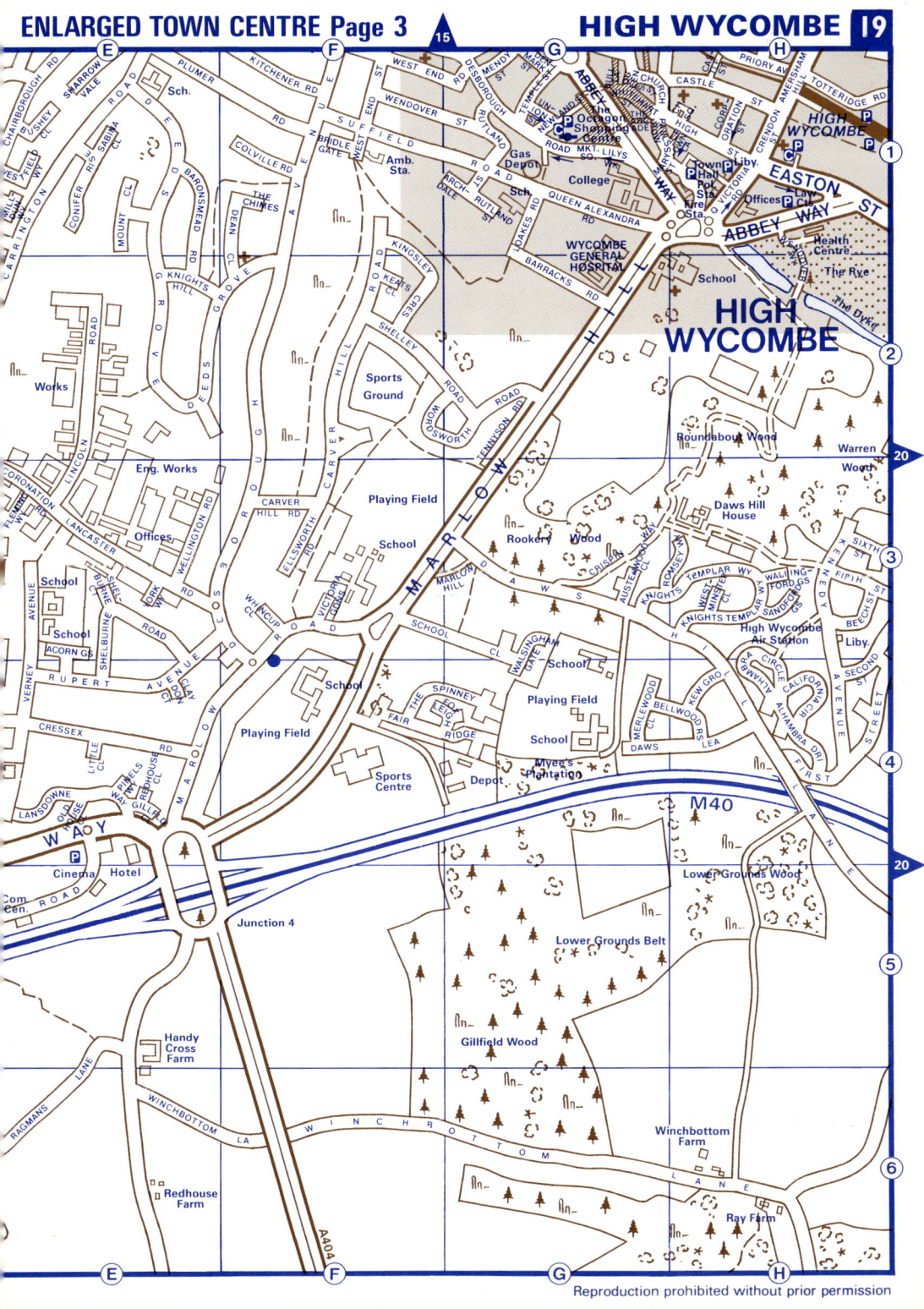

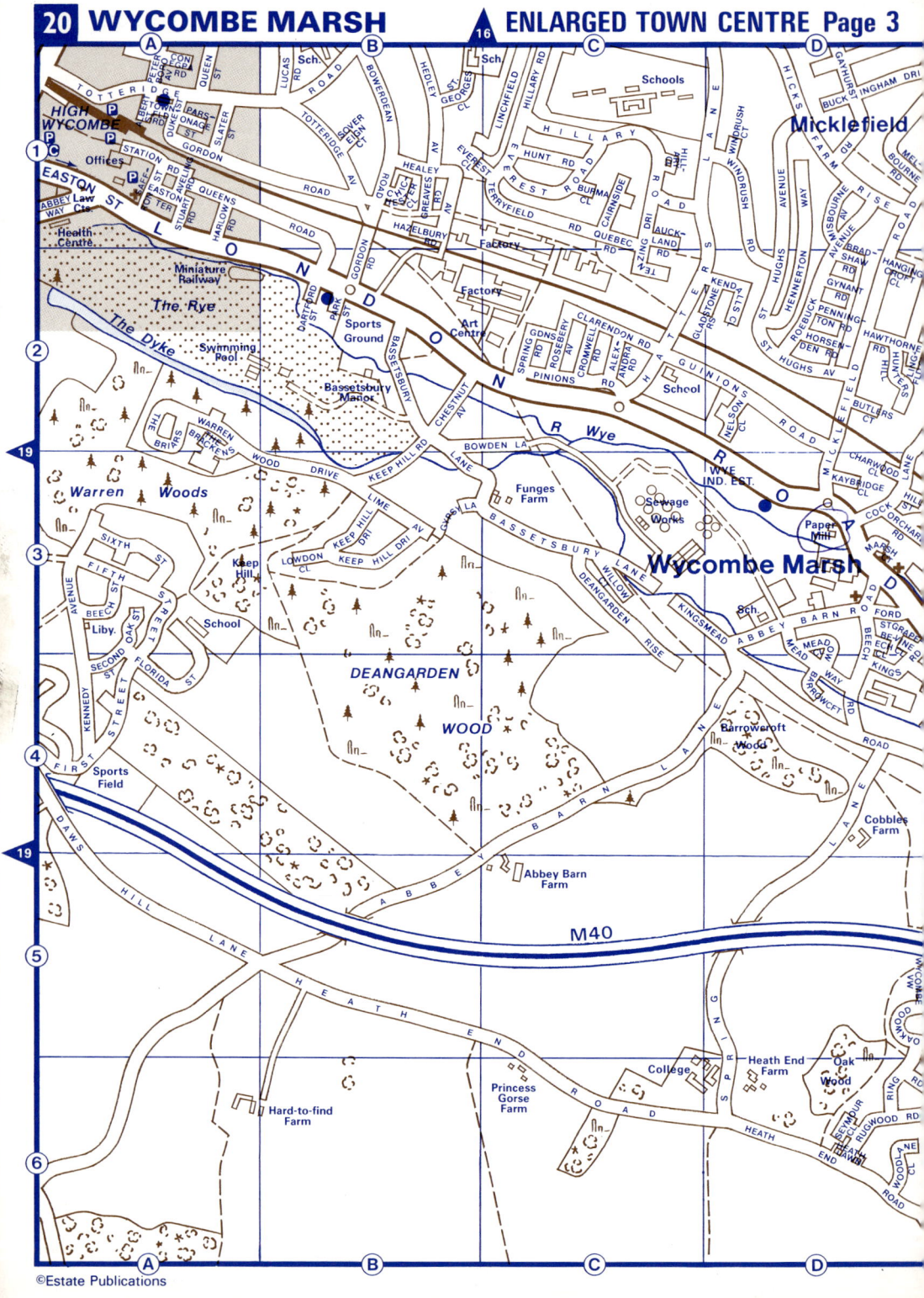

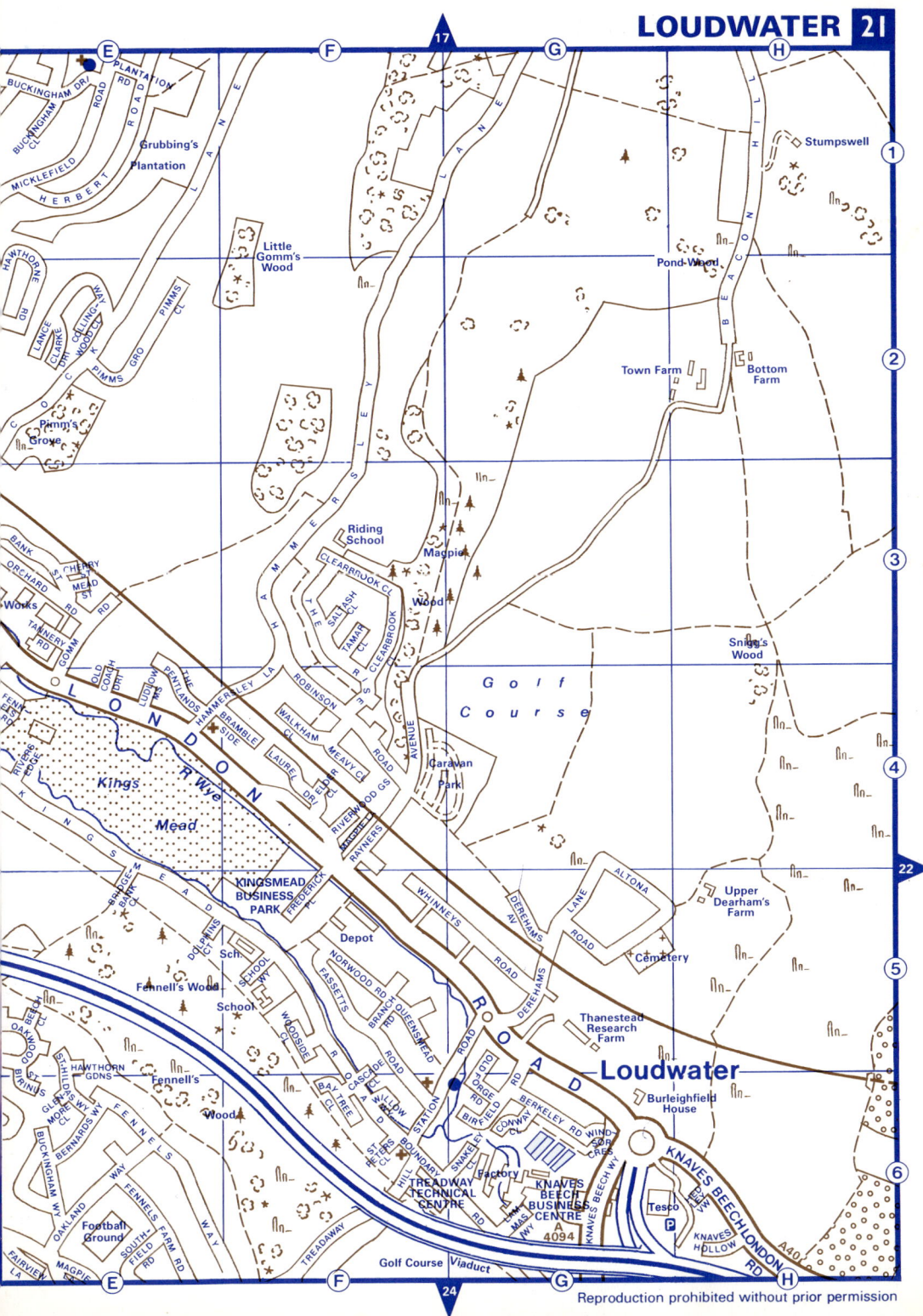

Gatemoor Wood

Corkers Wood

Baylin's Farm

Parsonage Wood

Coppice Hoop

Stander's Wood

Longfield Wood

Forty Green

Throshers Wood

Lule Farm

Roundheads End

Gomms Wood

Roundheads Wood

Hogback Wood Lane

Woodlands Dri

Woodlands Glade

Hogback Wood

Woodside Rd

Lower Wood

White House Farm

Whitehouse Tunnel

Holtspur Bottom Farm

Gregories Road

Stratton Rd

Cambridge Rd

Beechwood Rd

Chiltern Hills Rd

Hampden Hill

Caravan Camp

Holtspur

Cherry Tree

Rowan Cl

Burgess Wood Rd

Westfield

Cut-throat Wood

Holtspur Top Farm

Schools

Rec. Grd.

Ellwood Road

A40

White House

Highwayman's Farm

Cherry Tree Road

Chestnut Rd

Crabtree

Penington Rd

Burkes Cl

Wattleton Rd

Watery

WHITE HILL

M40

Heath Rd

East Way

Holtspur

Mayflower Way

Skelton

Fire Sta.

North Dri

OXFORD ROAD

South Dri

Barley Flds

Watery La

Old Moor La

Glory Hill La

Woodburn Green

B4440

Penn Road

Wychert Cl

Winchester Park

Wyngrave Pl

Rec. Grd.

Sch.

Seeleys Rd

Dower Rd

Seeleys Cl

Moss La

The Copse

Eghams Cl

Woodside

Woodside Rd

Baring Cres

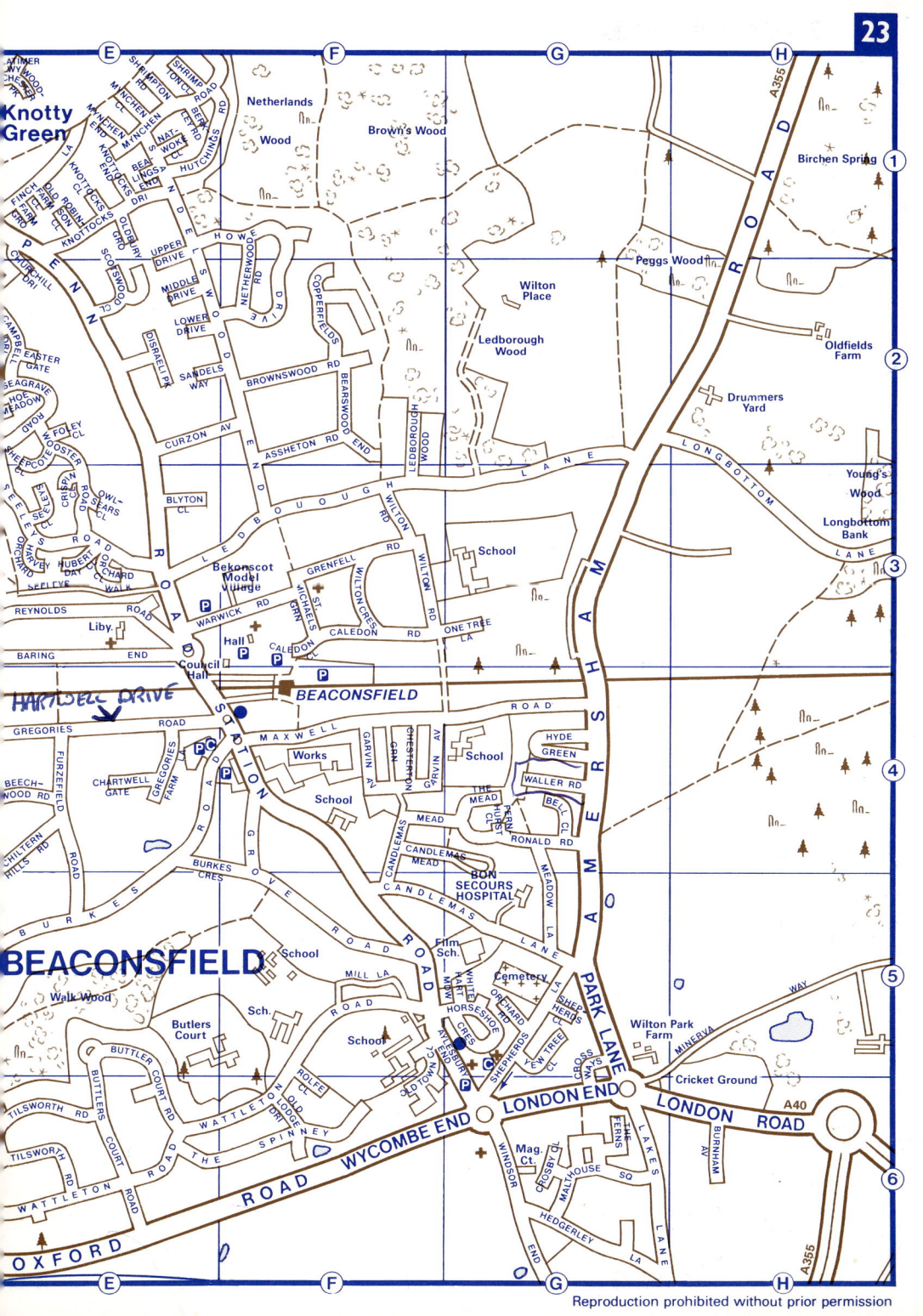

Knotty
Green

Netherlands
Wood

Brown's Wood

A 355

Birchen Spring
1

Peggs Wood

Wilton
Place

Oldfields
Farm
2

Ledborough
Wood

Drummers
Yard

LONGBOTTOM

Young's
Wood

Longbottom
Bank
LANE
3

School

Bekonscot
Model
Village

Council
Hall

BEACONSFIELD

ROAD

HYDE
GREEN

School

WALLER RD

4

HARTWELL DRIVE

Works

School

School

THE
MEAD
MEAD

FERN
HURST
BELL CL

Ronald RD

CANDLEMAS
MEAD

BON
SECOURS
HOSPITAL

CANDLEMAS

MEADOW LANE

BEACONSFIELD

Walk Wood

School

MILL LA

School

Butlers
Court

Sch.

School

Film
Sch.

Cemetery

SHEP
HERDS

YEW TREE CL

Wilton Park
Farm

5

WHITE HART MDW

HORSESHOE

CROSS
WAYS

Cricket Ground

A 40

MINERVA

WAY

LONDON END

LONDON

ROAD

A 355

OXFORD
ROAD
WYCOMBE END

Mag.
Ct.

WINDSOR

CROSBY CT

MALTHOUSE SQ

THE FERNS

BURNHAM AV

HEDGERLEY

LAKES LANE

6

E   F   G   H

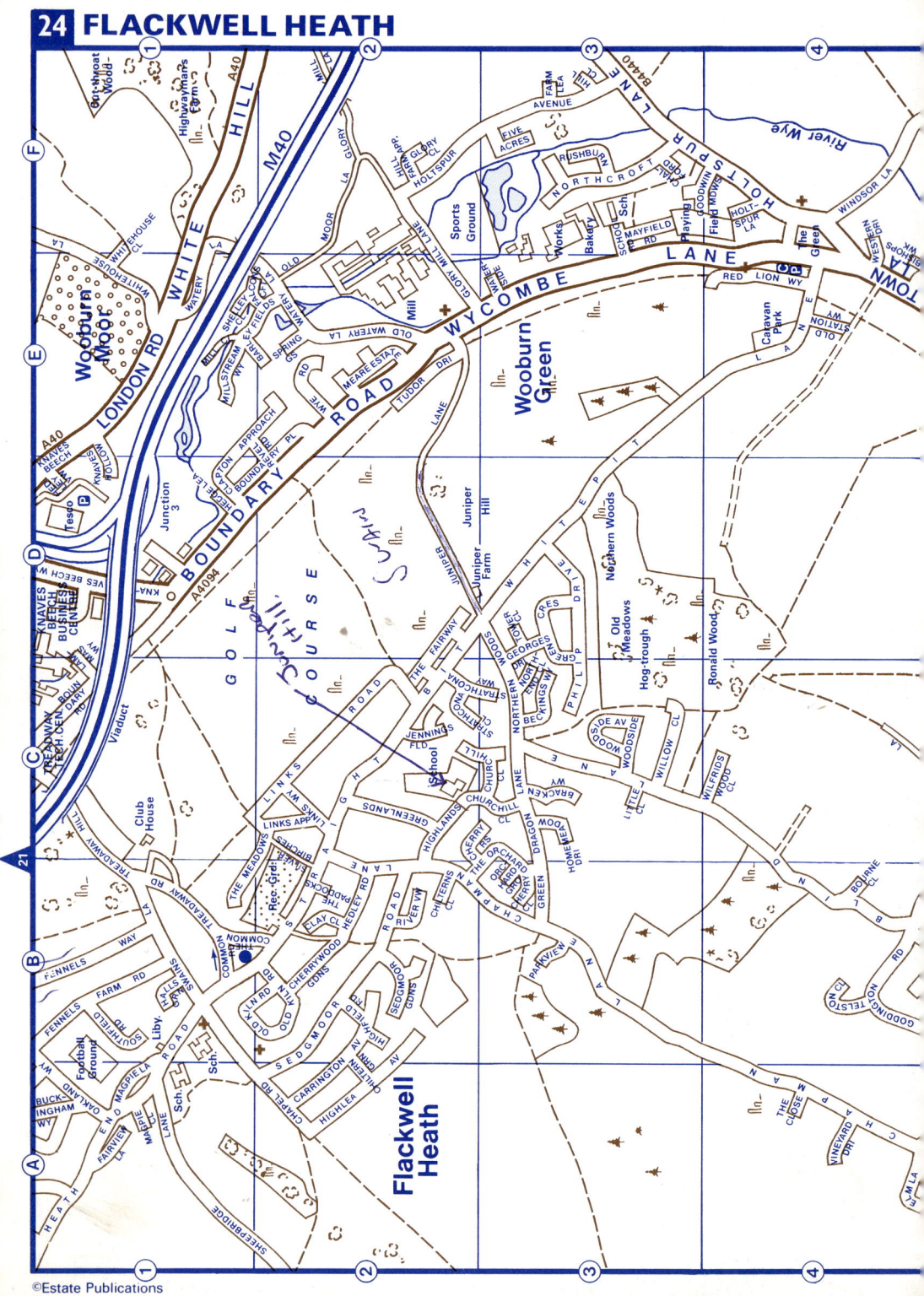

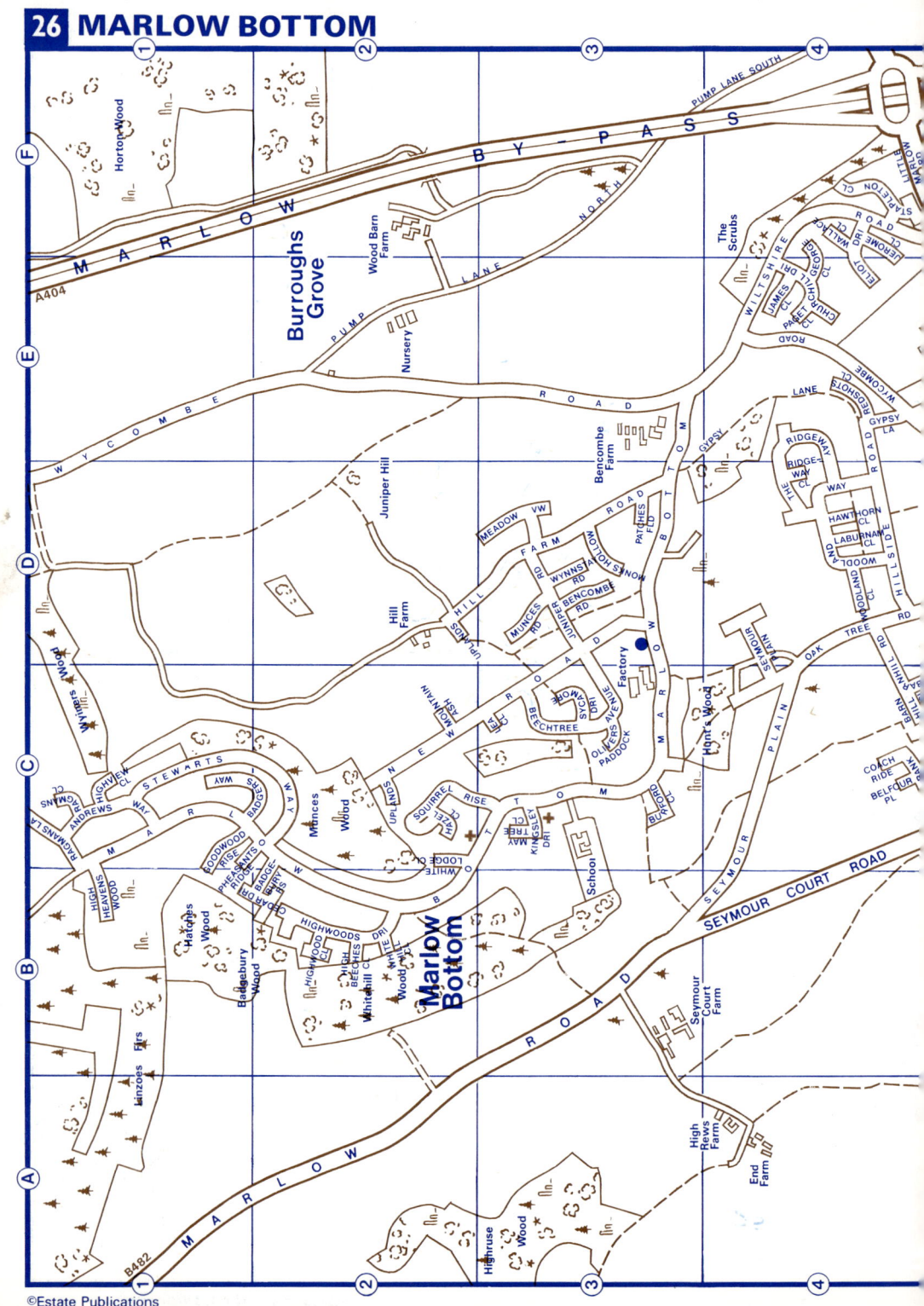

INDEX TO STREETS

Palliser Rd	8 A4
Parsonage Rd	8 B4
Pheasant Hill	8 B3
School La	8 B3
Seymour Rd	8 B4
Silsden Clo	8 C4
Silver Hill	8 B3
Stratton Chase Dri	8 A3
Stylecroft Rd	8 C3
Sussex Clo	8 B3
Sycamore Clo	8 A4
Sycamore Rise	8 A4
Sycamore Road	8 A4
The Brow	8 C4
The Lagger	8 A4
Town Field La	8 B4
Tripps Hill Clo	8 A4
Turners Wood Dri	8 C4
Upper Corner Clo	8 B3
Vache La	8 C3
Valentine Way	8 D3
White Hart Clo	8 A3
Woodbank Dri	8 C4

CHALFONT ST. PETER

Acrefield Rd	9 B6
Adstock Mews	9 C4
Amersham Rd	9 B1
Ashlea Rd	9 C5
Austenway	9 C6
Austenwood Clo	9 B5
Austenwood La	9 B5
Beacon Clo	9 C3
Benchmanor Cres	9 B5
Boundary Rd	9 B3
Bowstridge La	9 A2
Bull La	9 B6
Bywood End	9 D1
Cedars Clo	9 D1
Chalfont St Peter By-Pass	9 C4
Chapel End	9 B5
Cherry Acre	9 C1
Cherrytree La	9 B5
Chesham La	9 C1
Chestnut Clo	9 D3
Chestnut Walk	9 C3
Chiltern Hill	9 C4
Chipstead	9 A4
Church La	9 C4
Churchfield Rd	9 B4
Claydon End	9 C6
Claydon La	9 C6
Cleland Rd	9 B5
Copperidge	9 D1
Copthall Clo	9 D3
Copthall Cnr	9 C3
Copthall La	9 C3
Cordons Clo	9 C4
Criss Gro	9 B5
Croft Rd	9 C5
Cross Lanes	9 D1
Cross Lanes Clo	9 D1
Deanacre Clo	9 C2
Deancroft Rd	9 D2
Denham La	9 D1
Denham Walk	9 D2
Eleanor Rd	9 B4
Ellis Av	9 D4
Elms Rd	9 C3
Fernsleigh Clo	9 C2
Field Way	9 B3
Firs End	9 C6
Foxdell Way	9 C1
Garners Clo	9 D2
Garners End	9 D2
Garners Rd	9 D2
Glebe Clo	9 B3
Glebe Rd	9 A4
Glynswood	9 D2
Gold Hill East	9 B5
Gold Hill North	9 B4
Gold Hill West	9 A4
Grange Clo	9 C4
Grange Field	9 C4
Grange Rd	9 C4
Grassingham End	9 C3
Grassingham Rd	9 C3
Gravel Hill	9 C2
Greenfield Clo	9 D2
Grove Clo	9 A4
Grove End	9 B3
Grove Hill	9 A3
Grove La	9 A4
Half Acre	9 D4
Hampden Rd	9 B4
Hedgerow	9 D2
Hibberts Way	9 C6
High St	9 C4
Highlands Clo	9 D3
Highlands End	9 D3
Highlands La	9 D2
Hill Farm Rd	9 D3
Hill Rise	9 B5
Hill Rise Cres	9 C5
Hillfield Rd	9 C3
Hillfield Sq	9 C3
Hillgrove	9 D3
Hillside Clo	9 C2
Hilton Cres	9 C4
Hither Mow	9 C4
Holly Tree Clo	9 C1
Joiners Clo	9 D3
Joiners La	9 C3
Joiners Way	9 D3
Kingsway	9 C6
Lambs Croft Way	9 C5
Lansdowne Rd	9 B4
Latchmoor Way	9 B6
Laurel Rd	9 B3
Layters Av	9 A4
Layters Clo	9 A5
Layters End	9 A5
Layters Green La	9 A5
Leachcroft	9 A4
Lewins Rd	9 B6
Lewis La	9 D4
Lincoln Rd	9 C4
Linden Dri	9 C4
Llanbury Clo	9 D3
Lovel End	9 A3
Lovel Mead	9 B3
Lovel Rd	9 B3
Lower Rd	9 C4
Maltmans La	9 A6
Market Pl	9 B4
Meadowcroft	9 B5
Micholls Av	9 D1
Mid Cross La	9 D1
Milton Av	9 B6
Misbourne Av	9 C1
Misbourne Clo	9 C1
Misbourne Walk	9 C1
Monument Hill	9 C2
Morris Clo	9 D3
Narcot La	9 A1
Nicol Clo	9 B4
Nicol End	9 A4
Nicol Rd	9 A4
Ninnings Rd	9 D3
Ninnings Way	9 D3
North Park	9 C6
Northdown Rd	9 C2
Nortoft Rd	9 D2
Old Mead	9 C2
Orchard Gro	9 A4
Outfield Rd	9 B3
Oval Way	9 C6
Packhorse Rd	9 C6
Penn Gaskell La	9 D1
Penn Rd	9 B4
Pennington Rd	9 B3
Penshurst Clo	9 B5
Peterhill Clo	9 C1
Pinetree Clo	9 A3
Pond La	9 A4
Priory Rd	9 B5
Ravens Mead	9 D1
Rickmansworth La	9 C3
Ridgemount End	9 C1
Roberts Wood Dri	9 D1
Robinsons Orchard	9 C2
Robson Clo	9 C1
Royle Clo	9 D3
Russett Hill	9 D6
St Marys Way	9 C5
St Peters Clo	9 C4
Sandy Rise	9 C4
School La	9 B5
Scholars Walk	9 C2
South Side	9 B6
Southcliffe Dri	9 C1
Tate Rd	9 D1
The Dell	9 C2
The Drey	9 C1
The Drive	9 D3
The Greenway	9 B6
The Paddocks	9 C1
The Phygtle	9 C2
The Queensway	9 C6
The Ridgeway	9 C6
The Rowans	9 B6
The Vale	9 B4
The Warren	9 D3
Topland Rd	9 B3
Tunmers End	9 A4
Upway	9 D3
Vale Clo	9 B4
Weedon Clo	9 A4
Welders La	9 A3
West Hyde La	9 D3
Wheatley Way	9 C2
Wheelers Orchard	9 C2
White House Sq	9 C3
Windmill Rd	9 B3
Winners Clo	9 D4
Winners La	9 D3
Woodside Clo	9 C5
Woodside Hill	9 D4

CHESHAM

Abbotts Pl	4 D2
Abbotts Vale	4 D2
Addison Rd	4 D3
Albert Rd	4 D4
Alexander St	4 D3
Alma Rd	4 D3
Amersham Rd	5 C8
Amy La	5 C6
Appletree Walk	5 E8
Asheridge Rd	4 A1
Ashfield Rd	4 E3
Ashley Green Rd	4 E2
Aylward Gdns	4 B3
Barnes Av	4 D4
Batchelors Way	4 C3
Beechcroft Rd	4 B3
Bellingdon Rd	4 C3
Belmont Rd	4 C2
Benham Clo	4 C3
Bennetts	4 E4
Berkeley Av	4 A2
Berkeley Clo	4 B3
Berkhamsted Rd	4 D3
Bevan Hill	4 C3
Birch Way	4 E3
Black Horse Av	5 E7
Blucher St	5 C5
Bois Hill	5 F8
Bois La	5 F8
Bois Moor Rd	5 D7
Botley Rd	4 E4
Box Tree Clo	5 E7
Britannia Rd	4 D3
Broad St	4 D4
Broadlands Av	4 D4
Broadview Rd	4 C1
Brockhurst Rd	4 D3
Brushwood Rd	4 F3
Bury La	5 C5
Cameron Rd	4 D4
Cannon Mill Av	5 F7
Captains Clo	4 B1
Cavendish Rd	5 E6
Cestreham Cres	4 E3
Chalk Hill	4 C3
Chapmans Cres	4 B3
Chartridge La	4 A2
Cherry Tree Walk	4 E2
Chessbury Rd	5 B6
Chessmount Rise	5 E7
Chesterton Clo	4 C3
Chestnut Av	4 F3
Cheyne Walk	4 E4
Cheyney Clo	5 E6
Chiltern Rd	5 C8
Chilton Rd	4 D2
Church St	5 C5
Clay Acre	4 E4
Clifton Lawns	5 D8
Clifton Rd	5 D8
Codmore Cres	4 F3
Copperkins La	5 A8
Copsway	4 B1
Cordon Rd	5 D6
Cowper Rd	4 C3
Crabbe Cres	4 E3
Cresswell Rd	5 E7
Cross Meadow	4 A3
Crossway	4 F4
Danes Clo	5 C6
Darvell Dri	4 B2
David Walk	5 D7
Deansway	4 C3
Deer Park Walk	4 F2
Dellfield	4 B3
Delmeade Rd	5 B6
Dorney Rd	4 B3
Drydell La	4 A4
East St	5 D5
Elgiva La	5 C5
Elmtree Hill	4 C4
Elmtree Way	4 C4
Eskdale Av	4 D4
Essex Rd	4 D3
Eunice Gro	5 E6
Fair Leas	4 B3
Field Clo	4 F2
Five Acres	5 E6
Forelands Way	5 D5
Frances St	4 E3
Franchise St	4 D4
Freemans Croft	4 D4
Fryer Clo	5 E6
Fullers Clo	5 C6
Fullers Hill	5 A8
Garson Gro	4 B3
Gayton Clo	5 F8
George St	4 D3
Germain Clo	5 C6
Germain St	5 C6
Gladstone Rd	4 D4
Glenister Rd	4 D2
Grays Walk	4 C2
Great Hivings	4 B1
Greenway	4 C2
Greenway Par	4 C2
Halders Rd	4 E3
Hampden Av	4 B4
Harding Rd	4 E4
Harries Clo	4 C3
Hawthorn Way	4 E3
Hazelwood Clo	4 E3
High St	5 C5
Higham Rd	4 D4
Highfield Rd	4 C3
Hill Farm Rd	5 E7
Hillcroft Rd	4 C3
Hillside	4 B2
Hivings Hill	4 B2
Hivings Park	4 C1
Hodds Moor Rd	5 D7
Hollow Way	5 E8
Holloway La	5 F8
Holly Bush Rd	4 B1
Honeysuckle Field	4 D2
Hospital Hill	5 D6
Howard Rd	4 C2
Hunters Clo	4 B4
Inkerman Ter	5 E6
Kesters Dri	5 E6
King St	5 C6
Kirtle Rd	4 D4
Lansdowne Rd	4 D3
Larks Rise	5 E6
Latimer Rd	5 F7
Lindo Clo	4 C4
Little Greencroft	4 B1
Little Hivings	4 B1
Little Springs	4 C2
Long Meadow	4 D2
Longfield Rd	4 A3
Lowndes Av	4 C4
Lycrome La	4 F2
Lycrome Rd	4 F2
Lye Green Rd	4 E4
Lyndhurst Rd	4 C2
Lynton Rd	4 D2
Manor Rd	4 D3
Manor Way	4 E4
Market Sq	5 C5
Marston Clo	4 B1
Masefield Clo	4 C2
Mayhall La	5 B7
Meadow Clo	4 B1
Meads La	5 D6
Mill Clo	5 F7
Millfields	5 D7
Milton Rd	4 D4
Mineral La	5 D6
Missenden Rd	5 A6
Moor Rd	5 D6
Mount Nugent	4 B1
Nalders Rd	4 E3
Nashleigh Hill	4 D3
Nightingale Rd	4 C3
Nutkins Way	4 D3
Oakway	5 C8
Overdale Rd	4 C2
Park Rd	5 C5
Pargetter Clo	4 F2
Patterson Rd	4 C2
Pearce Rd	4 C3
Pednor Rd	4 A3
Pheasant Rise	5 E6
Poles Hill	4 B3
Pond Park Rd	4 C3
Poplar Clo	4 D2
Portabellow Clo	4 C3
Preston Rd	4 E2
Prior Gro	4 B4
Pullfields	4 B3
Pulpit Clo	4 D3
Pump La	5 F6
Punch Bowl La	5 D5
Queens Rd	4 D4
Rachaels Way	5 E8
Red Lion St	5 C5
Reynolds Walk	4 C1
Ridgeway Clo	4 C2
Ridgeway Rd	4 C2
Rose Dri	5 E6
Runrig Hill	5 F8
Russell Ct	4 E2
Ryecroft Clo	5 B6
St Leonards Rd	5 C5
St Marys Way	5 C5
Sayward Clo	4 E3
Severalls Av	4 D3
Shelley Rd	4 C3
Shepherds Way	5 E6
Short Way	4 C3
Springfield Clo	5 D6
Springfield Rd	5 D6
Stanley Av	4 C4
Station Rd	5 D5
Stoney Gro	4 E4
Sunnymede Av	4 F2
Sunnyside Clo	4 C4
Swan Clo	4 C1
Sycamore Dean	4 E2
Taylors Rd	4 E3
The Backs	5 D5
The Braid	4 F3
The Chase	4 C3
The Spinney	4 E3
Town Bridge Ct	5 C5
Town Field	5 D5
Townsend Rd	4 C4
Trapps La	5 E6
Treachers Clo	4 C4
Tweenways	4 F4
Upland Av	4 C2
Upper Belmont Rd	4 C2
Vale Rd	4 D2
Vale Road	4 D1
Valley Vw	4 C3
Victoria Rd	4 D4
Wallington Rd	4 C3
Warrender Rd	4 F3
Water La	5 C5
Water Meadow	5 C5
Waterside	5 D6
Webb Clo	4 C4
Wesley Hill	4 C4
West Vw	4 E3
Wey La	5 C5
Whichcote Gdns	5 E6
White Hill	4 D4
Whitehill Clo	4 E4
William Moulder Clo	4 A3
Windsor Rd	4 C2
Winstone Clo	5 C8
Woodcote Lawns	4 B1
Woodcote Wood	4 B1
Woodcroft Rd	4 E2
Woodland Vw	5 E6
Woodley Hill	5 E7
Wykeridge Clo	4 C1

GERRARDS CROSS

Amersham Rd	11 E3
Bakers Wood	11 H5
Beech Waye	11 E4
Bentinck Clo	10 B2
Birchdale	10 B5
Blacksmiths La	11 G6
Brokengate La	11 G5
Bull La	10 B1
Bulstrode Ct	10 C3
Bulstrode Way	10 B2
Camp Rd	10 B3
Chalfont St Peter By-Pass	10 D1
Cheyne Clo	10 C5
Coombe Vale	10 C5
Dale Side	10 C5
Denmead Clo	10 C4
Doggetts Farm Rd	11 G4
Donnay Clo	10 B3
Dukes Clo	10 C5
Dukes Kiln Dri	10 A6
Dukes La	10 C4
Dukes Ride	10 C5
Dukes Valley	10 A6
Dukes Wood Av	10 C4
Dukes Wood Dri	10 B5
East Common	10 C3
Elmwood Park	10 D5

Ethorpe Clo	10 C2
Ethorpe Cres	10 C2
Froggy La	11 H6
Fulmer Dri	10 B5
Fulmer La	11 E6
Fulmer Rd	10 D4
Fulmer Way	10 C2
Gaviots Clo	10 D5
Gaviots Grn	10 D4
Gaviots Way	10 C4
Hedgerley La	10 A4
Heusden Way	10 D5
High Beeches	10 B5
Hill Waye	10 D3
Hillcrest Waye	11 E3
Hollybush La	11 G6
Howards Thicket	10 B5
Howards Wood Dri	10 B5
Latchmoor Av	10 C1
Latchmoor Gro	10 C1
Latchmoor Way	10 B1
Layters Way	10 B1
Lower Rd, Gerrards Cross	10 D1
Lower Rd, Higher Denham	11 G4
Main Dri	10 B2
Manor La	10 B4
Marish La	11 G1
Marsham La	10 D2
Marsham Lodge	10 D3
Marsham Way	10 C2
Meadway Park	10 B5
Middle Cres	11 H4
Middle Rd	11 G4
Mill La	10 D3
Miller Pl	10 C2
Milton Av	10 B1
Mirrie La	11 G2
Moreland Dri	10 D3
Mount La	11 H6
Nailzee Clo	10 C4
Neal Clo	11 F5
Norgrove Park	10 C1
North Park	10 D1
Oak End Way	10 D2
Oakwood Park	10 D6
Orchehill Av	10 B1
Orchehill Rise	10 C1
Oval Way	10 C1
Over the Misbourne	11 E3
Oxford Rd	10 A1
Packhorse Rd	10 C3
Parkside	10 D1
Pinewood Clo	10 C4
Pinstone Way	11 F5
Raylands Mead	10 B2
Red Hill	11 G5
St Huberts Clo	10 D6
St Huberts La	10 D6
Side Rd	11 H4
Skylark Rd	11 G5
Slade Oak La	11 G1
South Park	10 D2
South Park Cres	10 D1
South Park Dri	10 D1
South Park View	10 D1
South View Rd	10 B1
Station App, Gerrards Cross	10 C2
Station App, Higher Denham	11 H4
Station Rd	10 D2
The Chyne	10 D2
The Glade	10 C5
The Uplands	10 C5
Top Park	10 B3
Uplands Clo	10 C5
Upper Rd	11 H4
Valley Way	10 B3
Vicarage Way	10 D3
Wayside Gdns	10 B4
West Common	10 B2
West Common Clo	10 C2
Windsor Rd	10 A5
Woodbank Av	10 B3
Woodhill Av	11 E3
Woodlands	10 D2
Woodlands Clo	11 E3

GREAT MISSENDEN

Abbey Walk	12 C4
Aylesbury Rd	12 B3
Back La	12 C4
Bernard Clo	12 B4
Broombarn La	12 A3
Broomfield Clo	12 A4
Broomfield Hill	12 A4
Chiltern Manor Park	12 B4
Church La	12 C4
Church St	12 C4
Elmtree Grn	12 C3
Frith Hill	12 C3
Great Missenden By-Pass	12 B3
Grimms Hill	12 A4
High St	12 C4
Hobbshill Rd	12 C4
Little Hollis	12 A4
London Rd	12 C4
Martinsend La	12 A4
Mill La	12 D3
Misbourne Dri	12 C4
Rignall Rd	12 A3
Robson Ct	12 B3
Station App	12 B4
The Garth	12 B3
The Square	12 C4
Trafford Clo	12 C4
Trafford Rd	12 B4
Twitchell Rd	12 C4
Upper Hollis	12 A3
Walnut Clo	12 C3
Whitefield La	12 C4
Winslow Field	12 B3

HIGH WYCOMBE

Abbey Barn La	20 B5
Abbey Barn Rd	20 D3
Abbey Rd	25 A5
Abbey Way	3 B2
Abbots Way	18 D4
Abercromby Av	15 E5
Acorn Gdns	19 E3
Acorn Pl	16 B5
Adam Clo	16 B5
Adelaide Rd	16 B5
Albert St	3 E3
Albion Rd	18 C2
Alexandra Park	3 B3
Alexandra Rd	20 C2
Alford Rd	18 C4
Alhambra Circle	19 H4
Alhambra Dri	19 H4
Alice Clo	13 E2
Allyn Clo	16 A5
Almond Walk	17 F2
Altona Rd	21 G5
Amersham Hill	3 D2
Amersham Hill Dri	16 A5
Amersham Hill Gdns	16 A5
Amersham Rd, Totteridge	16 A5
Amersham Rd, Widmer End	13 D4
Archdale	3 A3
Arinson Av	16 B4
Arundel Rd	18 B2
Ash Rd	18 C3
Ashdown Rd	17 E5
Ashfield Way	17 F3
Ashley Ct	17 F4
Ashley Dri	17 F3
Ashtree Walk	17 F3
Ashwell Manor Dri	17 F5
Ashwells	17 F5
Asney Court Dri	25 B7
Auckland Rd	20 C1
Austenwood Clo	19 G3
Avalon Rd	25 B5
Aveling Rd	3 F3
Avery Av	14 D3
Azalea Clo	17 E2
Bailey Clo	3 F1
Baker St	3 A1
Bank Rd	17 G5
Bank St	21 E3
Barbers Wood Clo	18 B3
Barbers Wood Rd	18 B3
Baring Rd	16 D6
Barley Ct	17 E2
Barleyfields	24 E2
Barn Ct	14 C6
Baronsmead Rd	19 E1
Barracks Rd	3 B4
Barry Clo	18 C4
Bartons Rd	17 E4
Bassetsbury La	20 B2
Bay Tree Clo	21 F6
Beacham Rd	18 C5
Beaconsfield Av	15 G4
Beaumont Way	17 E1
Beckings Way	24 C3
Bedder Rd	18 C5
Beech Clo, Flackwell Heath	21 E5
Beech Clo, Wycombe Marsh	20 D3
Beech Rd	20 D3
Beech St	20 A3
Beech Tree Rd	13 D2
Beechfield Walk	17 F2
Beechwood Rd	14 B3
Bellamy Rd	16 B5
Bellfield Rd	3 B1
Bellfield Rd W	3 A1
Bellwood Rise	19 G4
Benjamin Rd	3 C1
Benjamins Footpath	3 D1
Berkeley Rd	21 G6
Bernards Way	21 E6
Bevelwood Gdns	15 E6
Birch Way	17 F3
Birches Rise	15 E5
Birchwood Clo	14 D3
Birdcage Walk	3 D3
Birfield Rd	21 G6
Birinus Clo	18 C2
Bishops Walk	24 F4
Blenheim Rd	18 D3
Blind La	25 A5
Booker Hill Rd	18 C2
Booker La	14 D6
Boston Dri	25 B6
Bottom Alley	13 E3
Boundary Pl	24 D1
Boundary Rd	24 D1
Bourne Clo	24 B4
Bowden La	20 B2
Bowerdean Rd	16 B6
Bowler Lea	14 D3
Bracken Way	24 C3
Brackley Dri	13 C3
Brackley Rd	13 C3
Bradenham Rd	14 A1
Bradshaw Rd	20 D2
Bramble Cres	13 E3
Bramble Side	21 F4
Branch Rd	21 F5
Brandon Rd	18 C4
Brands Hill	16 B3
Brands Hill Av	16 A3
Brantridge La	25 C5
Brecon Way	15 E4
Brent Rd	25 B6
Briarswood	16 F2
Brickwell Walk	17 F2
Bridge St	3 A2
Bridgebank Clo	21 E5
Bridgestone Dri	25 C6
Bridle Gate	19 F1
Brimmers Hill	13 A3
Brindley Av	15 F4
Brook St	3 A2
Brookbank	25 D6
Brookfield Rd	25 D6
Brookhouse Dri	25 D6
Broom Clo	17 E2
Brown Rd	13 D3
Brunel Rd	15 E4
Brunswick Pl	16 B3
Buckingham Clo	17 E6
Buckingham Dri	16 D6
Buckingham Way	21 E6
Buckmaster Rd	18 C5
Bull La	3 C2
Burma Clo	20 C1
Burnham Clo, Bourne End	25 B6
Burnham Clo, Cressex	18 D1
Burroughs Cres	25 A5
Burrows Clo	17 G3
Bushey Clo	15 E6
Butlers Ct	20 D2
Butterfield	25 E6
Cairnside	20 C1
California Circle	19 H4
Calverley Cres	15 F3
Cambridge Cres	16 C6
Camden Pl	25 B7
Campbell Clo	15 F5
Campbell Rise	13 F2
Campion Rd	13 B3
Candytuft Grn	13 B3
Carisbrooke Av	18 B2
Carrington Av	24 A2
Carrington Pl	13 D2
Carrington Rd	15 E6
Carrs Dri	14 C5
Carter Walk	17 G5
Carver Hill Rd	19 F3
Cascade Clo	21 F6
Castle Pl	3 D2
Castle St	3 C2
Castleview Gardens	14 D6
Catkin Clo	18 B4
Cedar Av	13 B3
Cedar Ct	3 E2
Cedar Ter	15 F6
Chadwick St	16 B3
Chairborough Rd	18 D2
Chalfont Way	18 D4
Chalford	24 F3
Chalklands	25 A5
Challener Rd	18 C4
Chan-er Dri	17 F4
Chapel La, Cressex	14 C6
Chapel La, Downley	15 E2
Chapel Rd	24 A2
Chapman La	24 A4
Charwood Clo	20 D3
Chase Clo	17 F4
Chepping Clo	17 E4
Cherry Clo	24 B3
Cherry Gro	13 E3
Cherry Rise	24 C2
Cherry St	21 E3
Cherry Tree Way	17 G4
Cherry Way	13 C3
Cherrywood Gdns	24 B2
Cherwell Rd	25 B5
Chestnut Av	20 B2
Chestnut La	13 C4
Cheviot Clo	15 E4
Chichester Clo	20 B1
Chiltern Av	18 D2
Chiltern Ct	15 E6
Chiltern Grn	24 A2
Chiltern Pl	13 E2
Chilterns Clo	24 B2
Chilterns Park	25 B5
Chilton Clo	17 G3
Chippendale Clo	16 B4
Chorley Rd	14 A3
Church La	14 A3
Church Rd, Bourne End	25 D8
Church Rd, Penn	17 H6
Church Rd, Tylers Green	17 F5
Church Sq	3 C3
Church St	3 C2
Churchill Clo	24 C3
Churchside	13 E2
Clapton App	24 D1
Clarendon Rd	20 C2
Clarke Dri	21 E2
Clauds Clo	13 C4
Clay Clo	24 B2
Clay La	18 A6
Claydon Ct	19 E4
Clayfields	17 G3
Clayton Meadows	25 B7
Clearbrook Clo	21 F3
Clementi Av	13 E2
Clifford Rd	25 B5
Coates La	15 E2
Cock La	21 E2
Colbourne Rd	16 B5
Collingwood Clo	21 E2
Collyn Rd	18 C4
Colne Rd	16 D6
Columbine Rd	13 B3
Colville Rd	19 F1
Combe Rise	14 C6
Common Rd	24 B1
Common Side	15 E2
Common Wood La	17 G4
Conegra Rd	3 E2
Conifer Rd	19 E1
Coningsby Rd	15 H5
Conway Rd	21 G6
Cookshall La	14 B3
Copes Shroves	13 B3
Copners Dri	13 D3
Copners Way	13 D3
Copperfield	14 C4
Coppice Farm Rd	17 F3
Copyground Ct	15 E6
Copyground La	15 E6
Cores End Rd	25 B6
Cornel Clo	17 E2
Coronation Rd	18 D4
Corporation St	3 D3
Cotswold Way	15 E4
Court Clo	14 D4
Court Lawns	17 G4
Cowslip Rd	13 B2
Crendon St	3 D3
Cressex Rd	18 B5
Cressington Pl	25 A5
Cresswell Way	13 E2
Crest Rd	18 D5
Cricket Hill	25 C7
Crispin Way	19 G3
Croft Wood	16 D6
Cromwell Rd	20 C2
Cross Ct	14 D3
Cross Rd	18 D1
Crown La	3 C3
Cumbrian Way	15 F5
Curlew Clo	14 C3
Curzon Av	17 F3
Curzon Clo	17 F3
Cypress Walk	17 F2
Dandridge Dri	25 C6
Dartford St	20 B2
Darvills Meadow	13 E2
Dashfield Gro	13 A3
Dashwood Av	14 D5
Davenport Rd	18 C4
Daws Hill La	19 G3
Daws Lea	19 G4
Deacon Clo	18 B3
Dean Clo	19 F2
Dean Way	13 D3
Deangarden Rise	20 C3
Deeds Gro	19 E1
Delvin Clo	15 F5
Dene Wood	16 C5
Denmark St	3 B2
Derehams Av	21 G5
Derehams La	21 G5
Desborough Av	18 F3
Desborough Park Rd	15 E6
Desborough Rd	3 A2
Desborough St	15 F5
Disraeli Cres	15 F4
Dolphins Ct	21 E5
Donkey Dri	25 A6
Donwood Rise	15 H4
Dormer La	13 C2
Dovecot Rd	3 B1
Downs Park Rd	15 E4
Duke St	3 F3
Durley Hollow	15 H4
Earl Clo	15 G4
Earl Howe Rd	13 E2
East Dri	16 C5
East Ridge	25 C5
Eastern Dene	13 C4
Eastern Dri	25 C6
Easton St	3 D3
Easton Ter	3 F3
Eaton Av	14 D5
Edmunds Clo	18 C2
Edmunds Gdns	18 C2
Elder Clo	21 F4
Elder Way	17 E2
Ellsworth Rd	19 F3
Elm Clo	17 E2
Elm La	25 A5
Elm Rd, Booker	18 C4
Elm Rd, Tylers Green	17 G4
Elms Dri	25 C6
Elmshott Clo	17 E4
Elora Rd	16 C6
Estcourt Dri	13 A3
Evenlode Rd	25 B5
Everest Clo	20 C1
Everest Rd	20 C1
Fair Ridge	19 F4
Fairfield Clo	25 A5
Fairview La	24 A1
Falcons Croft	24 E2
Farm Clo	17 E6
Farm Lea	24 F3
Farm Rd	25 A5
Farndale Gdns	13 C3
Farrier Ct	25 B6
Fassetts Rd	21 F5
Faulkners Way	14 D2
Featherbed La	13 E1
Fennels Farm Rd	24 B1
Fennels Way	24 B1
Fern Walk	17 F2
Fernie Fields	18 C3
Fernside	13 C3
Ferry La	25 B8
Field Rd	18 C2
Fieldhead Gdns	25 B7
Fieldhead Home	25 B6
Fifth St	20 A3
Finch End	17 G5
Firs Clo, Hazlemere	17 F3
Firs Clo, Totteridge	16 C5
Firs Walk	17 F3
First St	20 A4
Firsview Rd	17 F3
Fishermans Way	25 B6
Five Acres	24 F3
Five Acres Wood	18 C2
Fleming Way	19 E3

Name	Ref	Name	Ref	Name	Ref	Name	Ref	Name	Ref
Flitcroft Lea	15 G5	Hawthorne Rd	20 D2	Wye Ind Est	20 D3	Lyndhurst Clo	14 D4	Ogilvie Rd	15 E6
Florida St	20 A4	Hayfield Dri	17 F3	Inkerman Dri	13 D4	Maclennen Pl	18 B2	Old Coach Dri	21 E4
Ford St	20 D3	Hazelbury Rd	20 B1	Isis Way	25 B5	Magnolia Dene	16 C3	Old Farm Rd	15 E3
Ford Way	15 E2	Hazlemere Rd	17 G2	Jackson Ct	17 E2	Magpie Clo	24 A1	Old Forge Rd	21 G6
Forest Way	17 E5	Hazlemere Vw	13 D4	James Clo	13 C3	Magpie La,		Old Harden Waye	16 C4
Forge Clo	13 E3	Healey Av	20 B1	Jeffries Ct	25 B8	Wycombe Marsh	21 F4	Old Horns La	18 B5
Four Ashes Rd	16 B1	Hearn Close	16 D3	Jennings Field	24 C2	Magpie La,		Old House Clo	19 E4
Fox Field	13 B3	Heath Clo	13 D3	John Hall Way	18 D4	Flackwell Heath	24 A1	Old Kiln Rd,	
Fox Hill Clo	15 H4	Heath End Rd	20 B5	Jubilee Rd, Downley	15 E3	Maitland Dri	15 H5	Flackwell Heath	24 B2
Fox La	13 D3	Heath Lawn	20 D6	Jubilee Rd,		Malmers Well Rd	3 D1	Old Kiln Rd,	
Fox Rd	13 D3	Heather Walk	17 E2	High Wycombe	15 F6	Malvern Cres	15 E5	Hazlemere	17 F3
Foxleigh	19 G4	Heathfield Rd	14 B6	Juniper Clo	17 F2	Manor Clo	17 E3	Old Moor La	24 E2
Frank Lunnon Clo	25 C6	Heavens Lea	25 C7	Juniper Dri	18 C2	Manor Gdns	15 G4	Old Station Way	24 E4
Frazer Rd	18 C2	Hedge Lea	24 D1	Juniper La	24 D2	Manor Rd	16 D2	Old Vicarage Way	25 E5
Frederick Pl	21 F5	Hedley Rd	24 B2	Katherine Clo	17 F5	Manor View	17 F3	Old Watery La	24 E2
Freemantle Rd	16 C3	Hedley View	21 H6	Kaybridge Clo	20 D3	Maple Clo, Cressex	18 D2	Orchard Dri,	
Frogmore	3 C2	Hedsor Hill	25 D7	Keats Clo	19 F2	Maple Clo, Hazlemere	17 E2	Cores End	25 D6
Fromer Rd	25 E6	Hedsor La	25 F7	Keens Clo	16 C4	Marigold Walk	13 B3	Orchard Dri,	
Fryers La	15 E5	Hedsor Rd	25 B7	Keep Hill Dri	20 B3	Market Sq	19 G1	Hazlemere	17 E2
Fulton Clo	15 G5	Hellyer Way	25 C6	Keep Hill Rd	20 B3	Marlow Hill	3 C4	Orchard End	13 C3
Furlong Clo	25 B7	Hennerton Way	20 D2	Kendalls Clo	20 D2	Marlow Rd,		Orchard Green	24 B3
Furlong Rd	25 B7	Hepplewhite Cres	16 B5	Kennedy Av	20 A4	Abbotsbrook	25 A5	Orchard Park	13 E3
Gallows La	14 C5	Herbert Rd	17 E6	Kennet Clo	16 B3	Marlow Rd, Cressex	19 E4	Orchard Rd	21 E3
Gandon Vale	15 G5	Hicks Farm Rise	16 C5	Kennett Rd	25 B5	Marsh Ct	20 D3	Orchard Way	13 E3
Garratts Way	15 F5	High Beeches, Cressex	18 C1	Kestrel Clo	14 C3	Marys Mead	13 B4	Overdales	16 D2
Gayhurst Rd	16 D6	High Beeches, Downley	14 D3	Kestrel Dri	13 D4	Marys St	19 G1	Oxford Rd	3 A1
George St	3 A1	High St, Downley	14 D2	Kew Gro	19 H4	Maurice Mount	13 B3	Oxford St	3 B2
Georges Dri	24 D3	High St,		Kiln Fields	25 E7	Maxwell Dri	13 C4	Parish Piece	13 D2
Georges Hill	13 A3	High Wycombe	3 C3	Kiln La	25 D6	Maybrook Gdns	16 A5	Park Farm Rd	14 C4
Geralds Rd	16 B4	High St,		Kings Ride	17 F4	Mayfield Rd	24 F3	Park La	17 E1
Gibbs Clo	15 F5	West Wycombe	14 A3	Kings Road	20 D4	Mayhew Cres	16 B5	Parkview	24 B3
Gibson Rd	18 B4	Highfield Av	18 C3	Kingshill Rd	16 B1	Mead St	21 E3	Parkview Ct	14 D5
Gilbey Walk	25 D5	Highfield Rd,		Kingsley Cres	3 A4	Mead Way	20 D3	Parsonage Clo	3 F3
Gillets La	14 C5	Bourne End	25 B6	Kingsmead Rd	20 C3	Meadow Clo	20 D3	Parsons Walk	13 D3
Glade View	18 B4	Highfield Rd,		Kingston Rd	16 B5	Meadow Walk	17 G4	Partridge Way	14 C3
Gladstone Rise	20 D2	Flackwell Heath	24 B2	Kingstreet La	13 F1	Meadow Way	25 B5	Pauls Row	3 C3
Glebe Clo	13 D2	Highfield Way	17 E2	Kingswood Rd	17 F5	Meare Estate	24 E2	Penfold Cotts	13 F2
Glebelands	17 G5	Highlands	24 C2	Kingswood Rd	17 E4	Meavy Clo	21 F4	Penfold La	13 F2
Glenister Rd	18 B3	Highlea Av	24 A2	Kitchener Rd	15 E6	Melbourne Clo	17 E6	Penmoor Clo	14 C5
Glenmore Clo	21 E6	Highwood Av	18 C2	Knaves Beech	21 G6	Melbourne Rd	20 D1	Penn Rd	17 E1
Glory Clo	24 F2	Highwood Cres	18 C1	Knaves Beech Way	21 G6	Mendip Way	15 F5	Penn Wood Vw	17 E3
Glory Mill La	24 E2	Highworth Clo	16 C4	Knaves Hollow	21 H6	Mendy St	3 A2	Pennington Rd	20 D2
Glynswood	15 H4	Hilary Rd	16 C6	Knights Hill	19 E2	Mentmore Clo	18 C2	Perth Rd	16 B4
Gomm Rd	21 E3	Hill Av	13 C4	Knights Templar Way	19 G3	Mentmore Rd	18 C2	Peterborough Av	3 F2
Goodington Rd	24 B4	Hill Clo	24 F3	Laburnham Dri	18 D2	Merlewood Clo	19 G4	Pettifer Rd	18 D2
Goodwin Meadows	24 F4	Hill Farm App	24 F2	Laceys Dri	13 C3	Merrydown	15 E4	Pheasant Dri	14 C3
Gordon Rd	3 F3	Hill Farm Way	17 E3	Lammas Way	24 C1	Micklefield Rd	16 D5	Pheasants Dri	13 D4
Gosling Gro	14 D3	Hill Howe La	13 D1	Lancaster Ride	17 F5	Middlebrook Rd	15 E4	Philip Dri	24 D3
Grafton St	15 E5	Hill Rd	14 A3	Lancaster Road	19 E3	Miersfield	18 D4	Philip Rd	16 B6
Graham Dri	18 C2	Hill St	20 D3	Lance Way	21 E2	Mill Clo	24 E1	Pimms Clo	21 E2
Grange Dri	25 D6	Hillary Clo	20 C1	Lane End Rd	18 A3	Mill End Rd	14 C6	Pimms Gro	21 E2
Grange Rd, Hazlemere	16 D1	Hillbottom Rd	14 B6	Langston Ct	14 D5	Millboard Rd	25 C6	Pine Chase	18 C4
Grange Rd,		Hillcroft Rd	17 G4	Lansdell Av	18 C4	Milldun Way	19 E1	Pine Clo	17 E2
Widmer End	13 A3	Hillfield Clo	15 E3	Lansdowne Way	19 E4	Millstream Way	24 E1	Pine Walk	17 E3
Grapevine Clo	20 D3	Hillside, Cores End	25 C6	Larch Clo	17 G3	Misbourne Av	20 D1	Pinels Way	19 E4
Gravelly Way	13 E4	Hillside,		Lark Rise	13 D4	Mole Run	14 D2	Pinewood Rd	14 C6
Grays La	14 D3	High Wycombe	16 B6	Larkfield Clo	16 D4	Moor La	14 D2	Pinions Rd	20 C2
Greaves Rd	20 B1	Hillside Gdns	16 B6	Larkspur Rd	13 B3	Mount Clo	19 E1	Plantation Rd	17 E6
Green Cres	24 D3	Hillside Rd	17 E4	Laurel Dri	21 F4	Mulberry Ct	13 F2	Plomer Green Av	14 D3
Green Dragon La	24 B3	Hillview Rd	16 B5	Lavender Way	13 B2	Mylne Clo	15 F5	Plomer Hill	14 D4
Green Hill	15 H4	Hinton Clo	15 G4	Lawson Rise	15 H4	Narrow La	15 H4	Plomers Green La	14 D1
Green Hill Clo	15 H4	Hither Croft Rd	15 E3	Leas Clo	16 D5	Neale Clo	18 D4	Plumer Rd	15 E6
Green Leys	14 D3	Hobart Clo	16 C4	Leigh St	15 F6	Nelson Clo	16 C5	Polidoris La	13 E2
Green Ridge	17 F5	Hobart Rd	16 B4	Lester Gro	17 E1	New Drive	16 C5	Pond App	13 E2
Green Road	16 A3	Hogg La	13 E3	Lille Clo	24 C3	New Pond Rd	13 E2	Portway Dri	14 B3
Green St, Hazlemere	16 D1	Hollis Rd	16 C4	Lilys Walk	3 C3	New Rd, Bourne End	25 B6	Prestwood Clo	14 D5
Green St,		Hollow Rise	15 H4	Lime Av	20 B3	New Rd, Cressex	18 C1	Pretoria Rd	3 F1
High Wycombe	15 E6	Hollyberry Gro	13 E2	Lime Clo	17 E2	New Rd,		Primrose Grn	13 B3
Greenacres La	17 E4	Holmer Farm Way	18 B4	Limmer La	18 B4	Tylers Green	17 F5	Primrose Hill	13 B2
Greenlands	24 C2	Holmer Green Rd	13 C4	Linchfield	16 C6	New Road Clo	18 C1	Princes Rd	25 D6
Greenside	25 B5	Holmer La	18 C4	Lincoln Rd	19 E3	Newland St	3 B3	Priory Av	3 C1
Grenfell Av	14 D6	Holmer Pl	13 E2	Linden Walk	17 F2	Newlands Mdw	3 B2	Priory Rd	3 C2
Grove Clo	25 D6	Holmoak Walk	17 F2	Lindsay Av	15 E6	Newmer Rd	18 B4	Progress Rd	18 B1
Grove Rd, Hazlemere	16 D1	Holtspur Av	24 F2	Lingfield Clo	20 D2	Nicholas Gdns	16 B5	Quebec Rd	20 C1
Grove Rd,		Holtspur La	24 F4	Link Rd	18 D1	Nightingale Clo	13 D3	Queen Alexandra Rd	3 B3
High Wycombe	14 C5	Homemeadow Dri	24 C3	Links App	24 C2	North Dri	16 C5	Queen Square	3 C2
Guinions Rd	20 C2	Honeysuckle Rd	13 C2	Links Rd	24 C2	North End Clo	24 C3	Queen St	3 F2
Gurneys Meadow	13 F2	Hornbeam Clo	18 C3	Links Way	24 C2	North Rd,		Queens Head	21 F5
Gynant Rd	20 D2	Hornbeam Walk	17 E2	Linnet Clo	18 B4	Four Ashes	16 B1	Queens Rd	3 F3
Gypsy La	20 B3	Horns La	18 B4	Lisle Rd	15 G4	North Rd,		Queensway	17 E1
Halifax Rd	18 B3	Horsenden Rd	20 D2	Little Clo	19 E4	Widmer End	13 A3	Ragmans La	18 D6
Halls Grn	24 B1	Hughenden Av	15 F4	Littleworth Rd	15 E3	Northcroft	24 F3	Ralphs Retreat	16 D1
Hamilton Rd	15 H5	Hughenden Rd	15 G5	Loakes Rd	3 B4	Northern Heights	25 B6	Ramsey Vw	17 E2
Hammersley La	21 E4	Hunt Rd	20 C1	Lock Bridge Rd	25 A6	Northern Woods	24 C3	Ravenshoe Clo	25 A6
Hampden Rd	15 H5	Hunters Hill	20 D2	London Rd,		Norwood Rd	21 F5	Rayners Av	21 F4
Hanging Croft Clo	20 D2	Huntley Clo	16 A3	High Wycombe	3 E4	Nursery Clo	17 G5	Rays La	17 G4
Hardenwaye	16 C4	Hylton Rd	14 C6	London Rd,		Nursery Ct	18 D2	Recreation Rd	25 B6
Harebell Walk	13 B3	Ilex Clo	17 E2	Well End	25 B5	Nursery La	17 G5	Rectory Av	3 E2
Harlow Rd	3 F4	INDUSTRIAL ESTATES:		London Rd,		Nutfield La	15 F5	Red Lion Way	24 E4
Harries Way	13 D3	Cressex Ind Est	18 D3	Wooburn Moor	24 E1	Oak Cres	18 C3	Redhouse Clo	19 E4
Hartwell Clo	17 G3	Desborough Ind Pk	15 E5	Longland Way	18 D2	Oak St	20 A3	Redman Rd	18 C4
Harvest Hill	25 D7	Jacksons Ind Pk	25 B7	Lorraine Clo	16 C5	Oakengrove Clo	13 E3	Redwood Clo	17 E2
Hatters La	16 C5	Kingsmead Bus. Park	21 F5	Lower Furney Clo	16 B5	Oakengrove Rd	17 E2	Rennie Clo	15 F4
Havenfield Rd	18 C3	Knaves Beech		Lower Lodge La	13 C3	Oakfield Rd	25 A6	Revel Rd	24 D2
Hawks Hill	25 D7	Business Centre	21 G6	Lower Ridge	25 B6	Oakland Way	24 A1	Reynolds Clo	16 C5
Hawksmoor Clo	15 G5	Marlborough Ind Est	15 F6	Lowfield Clo	17 E2	Oakridge Rd	15 E6	Richard Gdns	16 C5
Hawthorn Cres	17 F3	Rose Ind Est	25 B6	Lowfield Way	17 F2	Oaktree Clo	17 F3	Richardson St	3 A2
Hawthorn Gdns	21 E5	St Johns Est	17 F4	Lowson Clo	20 B3	Oakwood	20 D5	Ridge Way	16 A3
Hawthorn Pl	17 G5	Sands Ind Est	18 B1	Lucas Rd	3 E1			Ridings Cotts	13 E3
Hawthorn Walk	17 F3	Wooburn Ind Pk	25 D5	Ludlow Mews	21 E4			Ring Rd	20 D6

Ripley Clo 15 G5
River Vw 24 B2
Rivers Edge 21 E4
Riversdale 25 B8
Riverwood Gdns 21 F4
Robbins Clo 18 D4
Roberts Ride 13 B3
Roberts Road 15 H5
Robinson Rd 21 F4
Roebuck Av 20 D2
Roman Way 25 B5
Romsey Way 19 G3
Rook Rd 25 E6
Rookery Meadow 13 E2
Rose Av 17 E2
Rosebery Av 20 C2
Rosemary Clo 14 B4
Rosewood Gdns 18 C3
Rossetti Pl 13 E2
Roundwood Rd 14 C6
Rowan Av 16 B5
Rowan Clo 17 E2
Rowland Clo 25 D5
Rowliff Rd 18 D1
Rugwood Rd 20 D6
Rupert Av 19 E4
Rushbrooke Clo 16 D3
Rushburn 24 F3
Rushmoor Av 17 F3
Russell Way 17 F4
Rutland Av 18 D1
Rutland St 3 A2
Rydal Way 18 B2
Rye View 3 E1
Sabina Clo 19 E1
Saffron St 3 E3
St Andrews Clo 16 D4
St Birinus 21 E6
St Georges Clo 16 B6
St Georges Ct 14 D5
St Hildas Way 21 E6
St Hughs Av 20 D2
St Johns Av 17 F4
St Johns Clo 17 F4
St Johns Rd 16 D2
St Margarets Clo 17 G5
St Marys St 3 C3
St Peters Clo 21 F6
Salisbury Rd 16 B4
Saltash Clo 21 F3
Sanctuary Rd 13 D4
Sandford Gdns 19 H3
Sandpits La 17 G5
Sawpit Hill 13 C4
Saxon Ct 15 E5
School Clo, Downley 15 E3
School Clo,
  High Wycombe 19 F3
School Clo,
  Holmer Green 13 D2
School Rd,
  Tylers Green 17 G5
School Rd,
  Wooburn Green 24 F3
School Way 21 F5
Second St 20 A4
Sedgmoor Gdns 24 B2
Sedgmoor Rd 24 A2
Selwood Av 15 E2
Seymour Clo 20 D6
Shaftesbury St 15 F5
Sharrow Vale 15 E6
Sheepbridge La 24 A2
Sheepcote Dell Rd 13 F2
Shelburne Ct 3 E3
Shelburne Rd 19 E4
Shelley Clo 24 E1
Shelley Rd 19 F2
Shepherds Fold 13 F2
Shepherds La 13 B4
Sheraton Dri 16 B4
Shields Ct 17 F4
Ship St 3 A2
Short St 15 F6
Shrimpton Rd 18 C4
Shrubbery Rd 3 E1
Silver Birches 24 B2
Silverdale Clo 17 E4
Sixth St 20 A3
Skimmers Clo 13 E3
Skimmers End 13 E3
Skimmers Field 13 E3
Slater St 3 F3
Snakeley Clo 21 G6
Snowdrop Way 13 B2
Soho Cres 25 D5
South Dri 16 C5
South View 14 D3
Southbourne Dri 25 B6
Southcote Way 17 E4

Southfield Dri 13 C3
Southfield Rd,
  High Wycombe 14 D4
Southfield Rd,
  Flackwell Heath 24 B1
Sovereign Ct 20 B1
Spearing Rd 14 D6
Spindle Clo 17 E2
Spindle Ct 15 E6
Spring Coppice 18 A3
Spring Gdns,
  Well End 25 B5
Spring Gdns,
  Wooburn Moor 24 E2
Spring Gardens Rd 20 C2
Spring La 20 D6
Spruce Dene 16 D3
Spurlands End Rd 13 B1
Squirrel La 18 C3
Stanley Rd 14 C6
Station Rd,
  Bourne End 25 B6
Station Rd,
  High Wycombe 3 E3
Station Rd, Loudwater 21 F6
Steven Clo 13 D2
Stephenson Clo 15 F4
Stirling Rd 18 D3
Stockfield Clo 17 F2
Straight Bit 24 B2
Stratford Dri 25 D5
Strathcona Clo 24 C2
Strathcona Way 24 C2
Stretton Clo 17 F5
Stuart Rd 3 F4
Stumpwell La 17 H6
Sturgess Rd 13 C3
Suffield Rd 3 A3
Sunningdale Clo 18 B3
Sunny Bank 13 B3
Sunny Croft 14 C3
Sunters Wood Clo 18 C3
Sussex Clo 16 B4
Swains La 24 B1
Swallow Dri 13 C4
Sycamore Clo 25 C6
Sycamore Rd 18 C3
Sycamore Way 17 E2
Talbot Av 14 D3
Tamar Clo 21 F3
Tancred Rd 15 G4
Tannery Rd 21 E3
Taplin Way 17 F5
Taylors Turn 14 D2
Telford Way 15 F4
Telston Clo 24 B4
Temple End 3 C1
Temple St 3 B2
Tennyson Rd 19 G2
Tenzing Dri 20 C2
Terry Orchard 16 B5
Terry Rd 16 A5
Terryfield Rd 20 C1
Thames Clo 25 A6
The Arcade 3 C3
The Avenue 25 A5
The Brackens 20 A2
The Briar 13 E2
The Briars 20 A2
The Chase 17 F4
The Cherry Pit 15 E3
The Chimes 19 F1
The Cloisters 16 B3
The Close 24 A4
The Common,
  Flackwell Heath 24 B1
The Common,
  Holmer Green 13 E2
The Coppice 18 C3
The Crescent 16 C5
The Dell 17 G4
The Drive 25 A5
The Fairway 24 C2
The Glade 17 F4
The Green Acres 16 A3
The Greenway,
  High Wycombe 3 D2
The Greenway,
  Tylers Green 17 F4
The Haystacks 3 D2
The Homestead 18 D4
The Larches,
  Holmer Green 13 E2
The Larches,
  Tylers Green 17 G4
The Lavers 18 C3
The Lawns 17 F3
The Link 13 C4
The Meadows 24 C2
The Mid Way 18 D2

The Orchard,
  Flackwell Heath 24 B2
The Orchard,
  Widmer End 13 C3
The Paddock 18 B4
The Paddocks 24 B2
The Parade 25 A6
The Pastures 15 E3
The Pentlands 21 E4
The Pines 17 F4
The Quadrangle 16 C6
The Quadrant 16 C4
The Rectory 25 E7
The Rise 21 F3
The Risings 15 H4
The Rosary,
  Bourne End 25 A6
The Rosary,
  Holmer Green 13 D2
The Rosery 25 A6
The Spinney,
  High Wycombe 19 G4
The Spinney,
  Holmer Green 13 F2
The Thicket 17 E4
The Warren 13 B4
The Woodlands 17 E3
Thomas Rd 25 D5
Thrush Clo 18 C3
Tilbury Wood Clo 17 E3
Tilling Cres 17 E6
Tinkers Wood Rd 15 E4
Todd Clo 13 D3
Toms Turn 13 B4
Totteridge Av 20 B1
Totteridge Dri 16 C4
Totteridge La 16 C3
Totteridge Rd 3 E2
Tower Clo 24 D3
Tower St 16 B3
Toweridge La 14 A5
Town La 25 D6
Townfield Rd 3 F2
Treadaway Hill 21 F6
Treadaway Rd 24 B1
Trinity Rd 16 D2
Tucker Clo 16 B5
Tuckers Dri 13 E2
Tudor Dri 24 E2
Tudor Rd 17 G2
Turners Dri 16 C5
Turners Field 15 E2
Turners Pl 13 E3
Turnpike Rd 18 D4
Turnpike Way 18 D4
Tylers Cres 17 F3
Tylers Rd 17 F3
Tyzack Rd 16 C4
Underwood Rd 16 B6
Union St 3 B2
Uplands Clo 13 C4
Upper Green St 15 E6
Upper Hughenden Rd 15 H1
Upper Lodge La 13 B3
Upton Court Yd 25 C5
Verney Av 19 E4
Victoria Gdns 19 F3
Victoria Rd 3 D3
Vine Clo 17 E2
Vineyard Dri 24 A4
Waborne Rd 25 B5
Wakeman Rd 25 B6
Waldens Clo 25 A6
Walkham Clo 21 F4
Wallingford Gdns 19 H3
Walnut Tree Clo 14 C5
Walnut Way 25 B7
Walsingham Gate 19 G3
Walton Clo 16 C4
Walton Dri 16 B4
Warren Wood Dri 20 A2
Warwick Av 18 B1
Wash Hill 25 E6
Wash Hill Lea 25 E5
Watchet La 13 D3
Waterside 24 E3
Watery La 24 E1
Wayside 13 F2
Weathercock Gdns 16 B2
Welles Rd 15 E3
Wellfield 17 F2
Wellington Rd 19 E3
Wellsbourne Gdns 16 B3
Wendover Rd 25 A5
Wendover St 3 A2
Wendover Way 3 D4
Wentworth Clo 3 F1
Wessex Rd 13 C4
West Av 17 G3
West Dri 16 C5

West End Rd 3 A2
West End St 15 F6
West Hill 14 A3
West Ridge 25 C5
West Waye 16 B3
West Wood 18 C5
West Wycombe Rd 14 B3
Westbourne St 3 A2
Western Dene 13 C3
Western Dri 24 F4
Westfield Way 19 E1
Westminster Clo 19 H3
Westover Rd 14 D4
Wharf La 25 A6
Wheeler Av 17 F5
Whincup Clo 19 F3
Whinneys Rd 21 F5
White Clo 14 D4
White Hart St 3 C2
White Hill 24 E1
Whitehouse Clo 24 E1
Whitehouse La 24 E1
Whitelands Rd 14 D6
Whitelands Way 15 E6
Whitepit La 24 D3
Widmoor 25 E7
Wilfrids Wood Clo 24 C4
Willoughby Walk 14 D3
Willow Av 18 B4
Willow Chase 16 D2
Willow Clo 24 C3
Willow Walk 17 E2
Willow Way 21 F6
Willows Rd 25 C6
Winchbottom La 19 E6
Windmill Dri 13 A2
Windmill La 13 A3
Windrush Ct 20 D1
Windrush Rd 20 D1
Windsor Cres 21 G6
Windsor Dri 16 B4
Windsor Hill 25 F5
Windsor La 24 F4
Wingate Av 16 C6
Wingate Clo 16 C6
Winslow Gdns 17 E6
Winters Way 13 F2
Wooburn Manor Pk 25 F5
Wooburn Mews 25 F4
Woodcote Grn 14 D3
Woodland Clo 18 C1
Woodlands Clo 13 E3
Woodlane Clo 20 D6
Woodside 24 C3
Woodside Av 24 C3
Woodside Clo 21 F5
Woodside Rd 16 D5
Woodside Way 17 G4
Wordsworth Rd 19 F2
Wren Vale 15 G5
Wyatt Clo 15 F3
Wycombe La 24 E2
Wycombe Rd 13 D3
Wycombe Rd,
  West Wycombe 14 A3
Wycombe Vw 20 D5
Wye Rd 24 E2
Wynbury Dri 16 D4
Wyndham Av 15 F4
Wynn Gro 17 F2
Yew Tree Dri 13 B3
York Way 19 E3
Youens Rd 18 C2

LITTLE CHALFONT

Amersham Pl 8 B2
Amersham Rd 8 C1
Amersham Way 8 C1
Applefield 8 B2
Appleton Clo 8 A2
Arbour Vw 8 A1
Bedford Av 8 B1
Beech Park 8 A1
Beechwood Av 8 B1
Beechwood Clo 8 B1
Beel Clo 8 B1
Bell La 8 A1
Boughton Way 8 B1
Burtons La 8 B2
Burtons Way 8 B2
Cavendish Clo 8 A1
Chalfont Av 8 B1
Chalfont Station Rd 8 B2
Chandos Clo 8 B1
Charsley Clo 8 B1
Chenies Av 8 B1
Chenies Par 8 B2
Chessfield Park 8 C1
Chilcote La 8 A1
Church Gro 8 D1
Clayton Walk 8 B1
Coke's La 8 B2
Cumberland Clo 8 A1
Derwent Clo 8 A1
Elizabeth Av 8 A1
Farm Clo 8 C1
Finch La 8 A2
Harewood Rd 8 B2
Kenway Dri 8 A1
Kiln Av 8 B1
Latimer Clo 8 B1
Linfields 8 B2
Lodge La 8 D1
Long Walk 8 D2
Loudhams Rd 8 B1
Loudhams Wood La 8 C2
Maplefield La 8 A2
Maygold Walk 8 B1
Oakington Av 8 C1
Old Field Clo 8 D2
Pavilion Way 8 B1
Russell Clo 8 C1
St Nicholas Clo 8 A1
Sandycroft Rd 8 B1
Snells La 8 B2
Snells Wood Ct 8 B2
Stony La 8 D1
The Retreat 8 D1
Village Way 8 C2
Westwood Clo 8 C1
Westwood Dri 8 C1
White Lion Rd 8 A1
Yarrow Side 8 B2

MARLOW

Allanson Rd 27 F5
Andrews Way 26 C1
Archers Ct 27 D7
Badgebury Rise 26 C2
Badgers Way 26 C1
Barnards Hill 27 B6
Barnhill Clo 27 C6
Barnhill Gdns 27 C5
Barnhill Rd 26 C4
Beaufort Clo 27 D6
Beaumont Rise 27 D6
Beeching Stoke 27 F5
Beechtree Av 26 C3
Beechwood Dri 27 A8
Belfour Pl 27 C6
Bencombe Rd 26 D3
Berkeley Mews 27 E6
Berwick Clo 27 C5
Berwick La 27 C5
Berwick Rd 27 B5
Beverley Clo 27 E5
Bobmore La 27 E5
Bovingdon Heights 27 A6
Brampton Mews 27 D7
Bream Clo 27 B8
Brill Clo 27 B6
Burford Clo 27 E5
Butler Ct 27 F5
Byron Clo 27 F5
Cambridge Rd 27 C6
Caroline Ct 27 D5
Castleton Ct 27 D6
Cedar Ct 27 D6
Cedar Dri 26 B2
Chalkpit La 27 A6
Chapel St 27 D6
Charlotte Way 27 D6
Chilton Rd 27 C6
Churchill Dri 26 E4
Claremont Gdns 27 D6
Claremont Rd 27 D6
Coach Ride 26 C4
Conniston Ct 27 B6
Copse Clo 27 C6
Cresswell Row 27 C6
Cromwell Gdns 27 D6
Cromwell Rd 27 D6
Crown Rd 27 C6
Davis Clo 27 E7
Dean St 27 C6
Deanfield Clo 27 C6
Dedmere Ct 27 E6
Dedmere Rise 27 E6
Dedmere Road 27 E6
Douglas Clo 27 F5
Dukes Pl 27 E5
Edinburgh Rd 27 E5
Eliot Dri 26 F4